MEAT MANUAL

AUTHOR'S ACKNOWLEDGEMENTS
Thanks first and foremost to my wife, Kate and my daughter, Matilda. Thanks too to Louise McIntyre and all the team at Haynes. My thanks to my agent Antony Topping at Greene & Heaton. And finally thanks to you dear reader for buying this book.

© Andrew Webb 2016

First published May 2016

A catalogue record for this book is available from the British Library

ISBN 978 1 78521 077 8

Library of Congress control no. 2015958622

Haynes Publishing,
Sparkford, Yeovil, Somerset BA22 7JJ, UK
Tel: +44 (0) 1963 440635
Website: www.haynes.co.uk

Haynes North America, Inc.,
861 Lawrence Drive, Newbury Park,
California 91320, USA

Printed in the USA by Odcombe Press LP,
1299 Bridgestone Parkway, La Vergne, TN 37086

Author	Andrew Webb
Project manager	Louise McIntyre
Designer	James Robertson
Copy editor	Beth Dymond
Indexer	Derek Smith
Photography	Jamie Scott-Long
	shutterstock.com

MEAT MANUAL

From steaks to roasts, sausages to casseroles

Andrew Webb

Contents

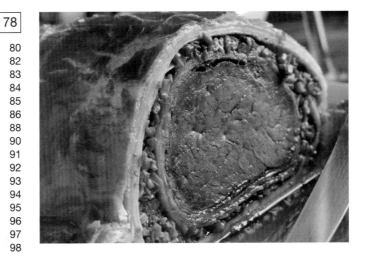

INTRODUCTION

Why do we eat meat? This might seem an odd question to ask someone who's bought this book. (You have bought it haven't you? You're not just leafing through it in a bookshop?) I suspect your answer might be something along the lines of, 'well, I like the taste, texture and flavour'.

The thing is, those attributes come in no small part from how that animal has lived, what it ate and how it's been handled afterwards. You can boil all this down to one simple statement: try to buy the best meat possible, as quite simply it'll taste better and have more flavour.

A long time ago, I made the decision to stop buying most meat, especially bacon and sausages, from supermarkets. Too many times I'd ended up with something bland and tasteless (beef mince), or swimming in fat (chicken and sausages), or covered in that weird white oozy stuff (bacon). I'd rather eat meat that actually tastes of something. To be fair, many supermarkets have upped their game in recent years, with 'dry aged' meat now on offer in some bigger stores, but I'm still wary.

SO, WHERE TO GET GOOD MEAT?

Well if you're lucky enough to live near a good butcher or farm shop, it should be your first port of call. If you don't know or have forgotten which cut of meat is best for which dish, talking to a butcher in front of other customers can be daunting. Remember though, that butchers want to help you. A good butcher will want you to go away happy so you'll return again; they're not out to fleece you. If they suggest something and it's out of your budget, ask them for an alternative.

It seems that within a generation or two we've forgotten how to talk to tradesmen (or women – there are some great female butchers out there too) but by asking them what's good, telling them what you're planning on cooking or how many you're feeding, you'll get the right piece of meat. Over time, you'll build up a relationship with your butcher – this is invaluable.

Today, we're not only seeing fewer butchers, but fewer animals in our day-to-day lives. In the past, many people often kept their own animals, particularly chickens, for meat.

(We did when I was a boy and this was in a suburban garden in Coventry.)

We can't wind back the clock to some halcyon rural idyll, because it never existed. Those happy-go-lucky peasants of old were just that: peasants, bitterly impoverished and forced to raise animals on scraps and eat every bit of them. Meat, for them, was a luxury.

Today, some meat is very cheap. We have 'burgers' made from carcasses of animals blasted with jets of water to produce a slushy slime that's then pressed into shapes, or meat injected with salty water to increase the weight under the guise of making it more 'succulent'.

The danger of becoming removed from butchers, farms and animals is that people can abuse the food chain. The horsemeat scandal of 2013 was meant to be a watershed in our relationship with meat. Of 27 beef burgers tested, 37% were positive for horse DNA (while 85% tested positive for pig DNA). One supermarket's value-range beef burger was found to be nearly one-third made up of horsemeat.

The other upshot is that some people are now scared of the visceral nature of meat: the blood, the offal, the 'bits'. I once knew someone who couldn't really look at mince until it was browned in the pan. They'd never roasted a whole chicken because they were too scared, preferring the occasional skinless, boneless chicken breast, which they then often smothered in spicy sauce – they might as well have been eating tofu.

But you're not like that – right? Thought not. Then this book is for you. It's a book about showcasing and celebrating high-quality, full-of-flavour, nose-to-tail, all-the-trimmings best of British, meat. So sharpen your knives and let's get started.

Andrew Webb
May, 2016

CHAPTER 1
TOOLS OF THE TRADE

The saying 'a bad workman blames his tools' applies as much to cooking as it does to any other activity. If you've not got the right equipment for the job, you're just making life hard for yourself. Not that you needs loads of expensive pans, plates, fancy Japanese knives or a state-of-the-art oven to cook great meat. So, before we begin the butchery, cooking and accompanying side dishes, let's first take a look around your kitchen and make sure you've got everything you need.

Knives

Meat begins at the sharp end. From the abattoir to the butchers, from your kitchen to your plate, it's all about the knife, and I cannot stress the importance of buying a really good one enough.

A good knife should feel weighty and balanced in your hand. When you first get it home, get some carrots and spend some time test-driving it, so you're comfortable and familiar with it, before hacking into expensive meat.

I'm a firm believer in the idea that a knife collection is something you build slowly, one piece at a time. I favour Zwilling/Henckels knives: a company that's been making knives in Germany since the 1730s. Hammer Stahl is a new company that makes some lovely knives too. Other people favour Global knives from Japan, while Heston Blumenthal endorses Tojiro. Indeed, many Western knife makers are producing Japanese-style blades now, which tend to be more slender. 'Santoku'-style knives are quite popular; this 'all-rounder' variety of knife comes from Japan and means 'three virtues', referring to chopping, slicing and mincing. They often have little scalloped holes running along the length of the blade; the benefit being that food is less inclined to stick to the blade when cut. The downside is that, due to the blade shape, they're not as 'rockable' (a fast chopping motion where you hold the tip of the knife with the palm of your other hand) as Western-style knives. Try a few out in the store before you buy.

Much like the top-flight Premiership football teams, there's probably very little difference between quality knife producers. There is, however, a world of difference between them and cheap, mass-

KNIFE CARE

CARING FOR YOUR KNIFE
Once you've bought your blade, look after it. A knife is for life, not just for Christmas! The quickest way to ruin one is to leave it rattling around loose in a cutlery drawer. It'll just get damaged, as indeed will your fingers if you leave it at the bottom of a sink full of dirty dishes.

A knife should be the first thing you wash up (don't put it in the dishwasher), dry up and put back in its box. Yes, that's right. Buy a knife that comes in a box and keep it there.

KEEPING IT SHARP
All knives will eventually lose their edge. You don't tend to notice this, as it happens so gradually. I sharpen my knives every few months; it's part of my 'Dadmin' (along with cleaning the car and going to the tip).

The two main ways to keep the edge on your knives is either by using a steel or a whetstone. A steel is a round bar with tiny grooves on that sharpens a knife when you repeatedly run it up and down it at the correct angle. To be honest, unless you're a chef and use one every day they're probably not worth the money.

It's far better to invest in a whetstone and sharpen your knives on that. It doesn't look as showy and 'cheffy' as using a steel, but you'll not have someone's eye out or lose a thumb and it'll actually get your knives sharper.

SAWS, FORKS AND TONGS

BONE SAW
Most butchery at home can be done with a good selection of knives. However, if you're sawing through bigger bones, such as a shin of beef (see page 85), then you'll need a saw. You can use a standard hacksaw blade from a DIY shop, but it'll soon clog up, as they have much smaller 'teeth' than bone saw blades, which are available online.

FORK
The advantage of buying a carving set is that it will include a fork with two large, long tines. This is for spearing the joint and keeping it still while you deftly slice the meat off using the knife. If you've not got one of these, use a set of tongs to hold the joint still – it's not as effective though.

TONGS
Still, tongs are great for many other meaty uses, such as adding steak to a red-hot pan or browning beef for a casserole. Ideally, you'll want two pairs: a metal pair for hard, hot work and a plastic- or rubber-tipped pair that you can use on non-stick pans without scratching them.

produced knives from the 'third division' you'll find in a supermarket. Be careful if you see a Sabatier knife for a bargain price, as many knife makers in France use that name; some are excellent, but many others are cheaper mass-market products.

COOK'S KNIFE
This is the workhorse of most kitchens the world over, taking on hundreds of everyday tasks, from cutting meat and slicing cheese to peeling large vegetables, such as squash. As well as a 15–20cm chef's or cook's knife, you'll also need a vegetable knife. Smaller, with typically a 6cm blade, these little knives are designed for more delicate work, often involving vegetables.

BONING KNIFE
If you're going to be doing significant amounts of bone removal, a boning knife is invaluable. These knives have semi-flexible blades that can follow the contours of bones and cut them loose from the flesh with minimal tissue damage. If you're boning out a leg of lamb or a chicken thigh, they're great. A flexible boning knife can also be used to fillet fish.

CARVING KNIFE
Most people today tend to carve with a normal 15–20cm cook's knife, but if budget allows, a carving set is a good buy. Carving knives have long even-length blades ending a fine point that make carving – particularly meat on the bone – a lot easier. The

trouble with a chef's knife is that it can get too thick towards the handle.

I have also experimented with a *cuchillo jamonero*: the long, thin, flexible knife used to carve thin slices of Spanish *jamon* (if you buy a Spanish ham for Christmas, they often come with one of these knives). They're not very good against anything too tough, or with bones, but if you've an 'all-meat' roast, such as a piece of topside or silverside, their fineness lets you carve off beautifully thin slices.

CLEAVER
Cleavers tend to cause more trouble than they're worth in a domestic kitchen. For a start, you need a really thick, solid chopping board to take the blows. Yes, they can cut through bones, but if you're not careful, you run the risk of a bone shattering and leaving shards in the meat. What's more, most bones can be popped apart at the joint.

They do look cool though, and if you've got the space and a huge wooden block to thump them into, go for it! The most awesome cleaver on the market has to be German manufacturer F. Dick's double-headed version, which is basically an axe for your kitchen!

BREAD KNIFE
The serrated edge of a bread knife is handy for, unsurprisingly, slicing bread. It's also useful for carving cold pies and other pastry work.

Chopping boards

Buy two big, thick, wooden chopping boards: one for raw meat and one for cooked items and other work. Like knives, wooden chopping boards are no friend of dishwashers, which cause the wood to warp, so it's out with the washing-up liquid and hot tap to keep these clean.

CATERING BOARDS

These are colour-coded as follows:

RED	Raw meat
BLUE	Raw fish
YELLOW	Cooked meat
BROWN	Vegetables
GREEN	Salad and fruit
WHITE	Bakery and dairy

For carving meat, I recommend a chopping board with grooves around the edges or down the middle, as a lot of fat and juice will come out of the meat.

I find most plastic boards don't come big enough for domestic use unless you buy coloured catering ones. Having one or two about to chop herbs on is fine, but for real kitchen work like butchery you'll need a large thick board that can take a pounding.

CLEANING YOUR BOARDS

A quick rinse under warm water and a wipe with a cloth is no good. You need very hot water, plenty of detergent and a lot of scrubbing. If you find your board starts to split or crack, it's time to replace it,

as bacteria love to hide in those dark, damp grooves. Once in a while, it's worth taking some sandpaper to your board to sand off any loose or damaged wood and get the surface back to being smooth.

USING YOUR BOARDS

A piece of damp kitchen roll, or better still a damp cloth placed underneath whichever board you use, will keep it from moving about. Also – and my old Home Economics teacher taught me this – keep a piece of old newspaper to the side of your board. You can then slide any trim, peelings or bits off onto the paper and ball them up ready for the bin or recycling box.

Roasting pans, trays, slow cookers

ROASTING PANS WITH WIRE RACKS

Buy something strong, metallic and sturdy with handles and with an internal wire rack that lifts your meat up out of the tray. This not only keeps your meat from stewing in its own juices and fat, but also allows the heat to get to the underside, helping it to cook. You can still place root vegetables and onions under the rack to help make the gravy.

If you ever find yourself roasting without a wire rack, use this tip: slice three large onions in half and stab a cocktail stick, pointing up, in each one. Place the sliced onions into the tray and force your joint or bird onto the cocktail stick 'spikes'. This should help keep it up out of the juices.

I own nearly a dozen roasting pans; all metal, as I think this conducts heat better. I do have ceramic dishes, but favour these for things you take to the table, such as a shepherd's pie or lasagne.

BAKING TRAYS

Despite their name, these are good for resting meat, cooking oven chips and various other everyday cooking tasks. Buy a few of these too – get good quality ones, as cheap ones can warp and buckle in the heat, causing their contents to spill.

YORKSHIRE PUDDING TRAY

These are critical for making individual 'yorkies' (see page 157). I prefer the shallow versions that produce a more rounded result, rather than the deep ones that you can also use for cupcakes or muffins that can give you something more, well, muffin-shaped.

SLOW COOKERS

Again, these were most popular in the 1970s – the idea being you just threw everything in, turned it on and when you came home from work your dinner was ready. You need to have plenty of liquid in there for them to work. They're very energy efficient, using no more electricity than a light bulb. However, I find that stews cooked in them don't really reduce like they would in an oven. Also – and this may be just me – everything comes out tasting the same. They're pretty good for making stocks though.

Pots, griddles and pans

Now, you've probably got pots and pans in your kitchen already, but below is a list of things that I've found invaluable, so plug any gaps in your pan collection. Your pans are going to take a lot of abuse over the course of your cooking, so get good ones. Plastic handles don't get as hot as metal ones, obviously, but can end up coming loose or melting if they're left over a flame.

MILK PAN

A small pan that's great for making small amounts of sauce. They often have a spout on each side for easier pouring. You only need one of these.

MEDIUM SAUCEPAN

A mid-sized all-rounder pan. Try to find one with high sides – this helps to keep things in if you're doing some frantic stirring. It's best to have at least two or three of these in the kitchen.

LARGE SAUCEPAN

This may still have a handle like its medium brother but it's better for boiling bigger things, such as potatoes or pasta.

CASSEROLE

This is a big pan with two side handles, which is as happy in the oven as it is on the stove. They come in a variety of styles, from the ceramic ones like your mum had in the 1970s, to metal non-stick and 'rustic' cast iron versions, which are heavy. I favour the latter, not because I think they look nicer, but I believe they can take more punishment. I've a battered old *Le Creuset* one I got in a sale; in my experience, though, other cast iron enamelled brands are just as good . Many casserole recipes call for browning the meat first; something that's not possible in many ceramic versions.

STOCKPOT

The bigger the better. I use a huge one that goes by the nickname 'Big Bertha'. It's also big enough for poaching or boiling meat, such as a whole chicken.

GRIDDLES AND GRIDDLE PANS

A griddle is any type of flat pan, often with low or no sides to it, unlike a frying pan. For meat, you'll want a griddle with ridges on it. These are more widely available now than they used to be, but beware of cheap versions that are little more than frying pans with tiny 'speed bump' ridges on. A proper cast iron griddle should be heavy to lift with deep ridges and high grooves.

The purpose of the ridges is to lift your meat up, allowing excess fat and juice to drain into the grooves. They also allow you to get the telltale lines on a steak (see chapter 4). The ridged griddle pan is a hybrid between a traditional flat griddle and a gridiron – the metal bars you would find over, say, a barbecue.

Another option is to do away with the 'pan' entirely and buy a cast iron griddle that you just place over the burners. The benefit of this is that you get much more room and can consequently fit more on. They're great for burgers and steaks.

FRYING PANS

Again, if you've got the space, a range of sizes helps. Little 15cm ones are great for quickly browning small amounts of meat, while having a large non-stick, high-sided sautéing pan with a glass lid is great for one-pot super-dishes, as well as sealing meat in larger amounts. I also have a third frying pan that I use only for fish.

STEAMERS

These perforated containers that sit on top of saucepans are good for cooking vegetables, such as broccoli and other greens. By steaming the vegetables to al dente rather than boiling, vegetables keep their shape and structure rather than turning to mush.

STICK OR NON-STICK?

I think you only need non-stick for gentle frying or sautéing; regular saucepans can be either. A griddle must be cast iron. Generally, non-stick pans are more delicate, and eventually – even if you never put a metal utensil near it – the non-stick coating does wear out. There's also been some health and environmental concerns around non-stick

FACT

The British Museum once displayed a fascinating Northern Irish griddle dating from the 1900s. When ships were built in Belfast (the Titanic was built there) the circles cut out of the hull for the portholes were sold as scrap. Often they were taken home and made into griddles for cooking items like soda bread.

Meat thermometers and other gadgets

OVEN THERMOMETER

See that small knob on your oven, the size of your thumb? Turning that changes your oven from room temperature to around 230°C in just three-quarters of a turn. This makes most ovens very inaccurate at precise temperature measurement, which can affect your cooking.

Even if you've got a digital display fan oven, you're still beholden to where the thermostat is situated, which is normally towards the back of the oven. My oven typically runs hotter to the front right-hand side. The point is, it's important to know what's going on and where the action is. So is being able to see in the thing, so if your oven door's a little grubby, get out the scouring pads and give the glass a really good scrub.

MEAT THERMOMETER

A better way to measure temperature is to buy a digital meat thermometer. These handy things cost less than a fiver and have a temperature range of 50–300°C. You need to ensure that you always insert the tip into the centre of the thickest part of the meat. If it pushes through to the other side you'll get a false reading. You can also use them for measuring the temperature of oil for deep frying, baking and seeing if the kids have a fever!

BUTCHERS' TWINE

This is string for tying up joints. Learning to tie this properly takes real butcher's skill.

FLAVOUR INJECTOR

I've used these to inject pureed garlic into a leg of lamb (see page 115) as well as pineapple juice into a shoulder of pork. You can also use them to quick-brine chicken (see page 28). If you've a fear of needles this giant syringe is your worst nightmare.

CRAFT OR STANLEY KNIFE

These are, I think, invaluable for slashing pork skin to make crackling.

MEAT GLUE

Yes, that's right, glue for meat! Or to give it its technical and less weird-sounding name; transglutaminase. It's an enzyme with the ability to cross-link proteins – effectively sticking them together – meaning that you can build terrines and seal stuffed chicken breasts easily. It has no taste, so it won't spoil your meat.

STEAK TENDERISER

Rewind to the 1970s and anyone hoping to woo a potential date with home-cooked dishes, like steak Diane or veal escalope, would first pound said steaks with a mallet. Yet you'd be hard pressed to find such an item in most kitchen shops these days. To be honest, I don't think they're worth the money; if you do need to flatten or tenderise a steak, a rolling pin is probably just as good.

MEAT AND POULTRY LIFTERS

If you roast a lot of chicken, then you might want to consider buying a pair of these. They're basically two large forks that enable you to stab and lift meat. I find a pair of tongs can lift most chickens, but if you're dealing with turkey or any larger pieces of meat, these do help. Poultry shears are also a waste of money, in my opinion.

BASTER

This, basically, is a giant pipette that you use to lift fat and juice from the bottom of the pan to dribble it over the top of the meat. It can also be used for removing excess fat. To be honest, you can do the same thing with a spoon.

GRAVY SEPARATOR

This clever jug is ace for removing fat from your gravy and pan juices. You pour in the contents of the roasting pan and the fat rises to the top. The spout, however, starts at the bottom, which allows you to pour off the gravy. You can pick them up cheaply.

If you ever find yourself without a gravy separator, try this simple trick: get your tallest mug and put it in the freezer before you start to roast you meat. While the meat's resting, pour the pan juices and fat into the frozen mug and put it back in the freezer. After about 15 minutes, the fat should have solidified enough for you to remove most of it with a spoon. You can then pour the separated gravy back into a saucepan to reheat.

BRANDING IRON

Finally, the ultimate meat gadget has to be your own custom-made branding iron to sear your steaks. Eyre and Baxter are a Sheffield-based company that make custom branding irons: www.eyreandbaxter.co.uk.

Correct oven and hob use

Go into your kitchen and take a look at your oven and hob in the cold light of day. Could they, perhaps, do with a clean? Has the bulb gone in the oven? Do all the burners fire up correctly? Ovens are a once-a-decade purchase, if that – indeed you're probably more likely to get to experience a 'new' oven by splitting up and moving out than you are by buying a new one.

THE HOB

Most of your meat cooking will be on your hob. Even things that later end up in the oven, like joints or stews, are often sealed first in a pan. You've probably got a big burner, two medium ones and a small one. Needless to say, the big one heats things fastest, so use this one for getting your griddle pan smoking hot or for when you're sealing meat. The medium ones are all-rounders, and the small one is best used for milk pans and making coffee.

THE OVEN

Technically, meat cooked in today's ovens is baked rather than roasted. If you've ever been lucky enough to try beef roasted directly in front of an open fire, you'll know what I'm talking about. So, the little we lose in flavour and texture, we more than make up for in safety and convenience.

It's something that we don't really think about, but cooking accounts for about 4% of the average gas and electricity bill. Here are some tips not only to save money, but also to improve your meat cooking:

- Cook in batches: it requires a bit of thinking ahead and, perhaps, following two recipes at the same time, but cooking a number of meals at once means you'll have food to freeze or eat later.
- Use saucepan lids: liquids come to the boil much faster, using less energy.

- Don't open the oven door too much: this causes the oven to lose heat and the internal temperature to drop.
- Turn the oven off around 10–15 minutes before the end of the cooking time: it'll still be hot enough in there to continue cooking, but you won't be using any energy.
- Finally, you can bake or prove bread in a cooling oven.

OVEN GLOVES

Get yourself a big, thick pair of oven gloves. I tend to favour two mitts with a long sleeve, rather than those 'handcuff' types. Worth shelling out a few extra quid here, even if you've got asbestos hands. You don't want to drop your roasted meat because the tray's too hot.

HEAT LEVELS FOR LIQUIDS

- **Rapid boil** – Lots of bubbles, with the heat as quickly applied as your stove can manage. Cooks small things very fast; often you bring things to this point and them drop down to…
- **Rolling boil** – Bubbles seemingly turning over themselves. This is much better for poaching meat and cooking vegetables or pasta.
- **Simmer** – Best applied to non-water-based liquids. Simmering slowly reduces a liquid by volume by evaporating the water element, leaving a concentrated flavour. This is good for sauces.
- **Ticking over** – Finally, there's what I call 'barely ticking over': this is used for very long and slow poaching, and for making stocks. It's as low a heat as your cooker can do, and is best used on large pots of liquid.

Oven temperatures

A word about oven temperatures in this book. Nearly everyone these days has a fan-assisted oven measured in degrees Celsius, so all the cooking times are given for that. If you've not got a fan oven, up the temperature by about 20°C; if you're using gas, see the conversion tables on page 173.

Raw meat and kitchen hygiene

The very first thing you should do when cooking is wash your hands. According to research carried out by Queen Mary, University of London and the London School of Hygiene & Tropical Medicine, the average person's hands host at least 3,000 different bacteria belonging to more than 100 species. What's more, women (who wash their hands more than men) have a more diverse selection of germs living on them. Scientists don't know why.

'The first and most important [thing] is cleanliness, not only in their own persons but also in every article used.' That is the opening line of Francis Collingwood's *The Universal Cook*, and it's as true today as it was when written in 1792.

Always keep raw meat at the bottom of the fridge

Never wash poultry, you're just splashing bacteria on your worktop

CHICKEN

Let's start with chicken. It's an outrage that, according to the Food Standards Agency, 73% of poultry in the UK is contaminated with the bacteria campylobacter, the most common cause of food poisoning in the UK. You can't see it, smell it or taste it, but if it gets inside you… well, let's just say things won't stay inside for very long! Symptoms include abdominal pain, severe diarrhoea and, occasionally, vomiting – it's nasty.

Until our factory-farming system sorts itself out and eradicates campylobacter, the onus is on us – the consumer – to stop it spreading. Thankfully, the cooking process kills it easily and you can keep it out of your kitchen by following this advice:

- Store raw chicken separately from other food; covered or wrapped on the bottom shelf of your fridge. Put any packaging straight in the bin, as the Food Standards Agency survey also found that 7% of chicken packaging tested positive for the presence of campylobacter.
- Don't wash raw chicken: it can splash bacteria around your kitchen.
- Wash everything – all hands, knives, utensils and chopping boards that have touched raw chicken – with detergent or kitchen cleaner and hot water. Also, don't do things like open cupboards with 'raw' hands; you can leave bacteria on the handles and surfaces. Do any raw preparation either first, and then completely clean down all surfaces and utensils, or last, after you've done all the other things. What you don't want is to be breaking apart raw chicken next to a bowl of salad!
- Check chicken is cooked through: this is not a meat to serve rare. If there's any pinkness to the flesh or the juices, it's back in the oven. The thighs and breast are the thickest parts of the bird and so the heat will take longer to penetrate there. That's the place to poke with your meat thermometer.
- To destroy any campylobacter or salmonella, you need an internal temperature of 60°C for 10 minutes (it's actually a little less for campylobacter). To be on the safe side, the general advice is to heat to a temperature of 73–75°C for 10 minutes.
- It's best to treat all feathered game in the same way as chicken.

BEEF AND LAMB

Raw beef, lamb and furred game such as venison should all be kept covered in the lowest part of the fridge. The rules about chopping boards also apply. Whole cuts, such as chops and steaks can be served rare, as any viral contamination should only be on the outside and will be destroyed during the cooking process.

The Food Standards Agency's advice for dishes made with minced meat, such as burgers, sausages and kebabs, is to cook them all thoroughly. Due to their minced-up nature, any contamination on the outside can find itself on the inside. However, if you've ever eaten a well-done burger, you'll know what a dispiriting experience it is chewing on a rubbery hockey puck! Sausages should always be cooked through, however.

PORK

In the past, pork suffered from what chicken is going through now, with mass-produced, factory-farmed meat becoming infected with trichinosis (a disease caused by the larvae of a small nematode worm – yum!). Pork producers stopped feeding contaminated feed to pigs and worked hard to stamp out the infection. However, current Food Standards Agency advice is to cook pork all the way through to an internal temperature of 70°C.

A few years ago, the US Department of Agriculture revised their guidance for cooking pork, recommending that the internal temperature should reach 62°C with a three-minute rest time, and there are some chefs who like to serve their pork 'juicy'. To be clear, this isn't rare like beef. I think you've got to be really careful here and wouldn't recommend it, especially if you've young, pregnant or elderly guests.

In the heat of cooking, it's easy to forget about hygiene and proper kitchen best practice, but all your culinary efforts are worthless if you and your guests get food poisoning, so keep it clean.

WHAT'S THE DIRTIEST THING IN YOUR HOUSE?

It's got to be your toilet – right? I mean, think of what goes in it! Wrong. A study from the University of Arizona found that on average, a toilet seat is home to around 50 bacteria per square inch. That's pretty clean compared to a kitchen chopping board, which might host 200 times that. E. coli and staphylococcus aureus get on your chopping board via raw meat, which has often come into contact with the organs from inside the animal.

The worst culprit, however, is the kitchen sponge or dishcloth. There are about 10 million bacteria per square inch on a sponge and a million on a dishcloth, meaning a kitchen sponge is 200,000 times dirtier than a toilet seat and a dishcloth is 20,000 times dirtier! The moral of this story is, replace that cloth or sponge regularly. Sponges can be put in the dishwasher to sterilise them, while dishcloths can go in with the laundry.

HOW MANY TIMES CAN I REHEAT MEAT?

You should only reheat or re-cook meat once. So, say you've some leftover lamb that you mince to make two small shepherd's pies: one for today and one for the freezer. The first pie will be fine, having only been reheated once. The second, however, would contain meat that will be reheated twice: once for the cooking of the shepherd's pie and once when you get it out of the freezer.

Cooking meat over fire

Meat, meet fire. This momentous introduction is thought to have taken place around one million years ago. Cooking meat makes it easier to chew and digest; it also makes it tasty, really tasty. And so much like being able to ride a horse, humans have been cooking meat over a fire for a long time. Then, in the last century, both those skills were seemingly lost in a generation or two. Today, all we have left is the barbecue.

There was a time when us Brits didn't really get barbecuing or cooking outdoors in general. Of course, historically we've cooked over or in front of flames, but that's not quite barbecuing. In his book, *Barbecue: The History of an American Institution*, Robert F. Moss describes British colonists adopting barbecuing techniques from Native Americans in the 16th and 17th centuries. This style was then transferred to other parts of the Empire, such as South Africa and Australia. But it never really made it back to Britain – blame the weather.

Then, in the past five years, there's been an explosion of 'dude food' and the USA style of outdoor cooking with less flame and longer cooking times: so-called, 'low and slow'. Consequently, many of our cities are now awash with burgers, ribs, smoked this and pulled that. The US isn't the only nation with a culture of outdoor cooking, however; South America, southern Asia and the Caribbean all have variations.

CHARCOAL BARBECUES

The late, great food writer and founder of Meatopia, Josh Ozersky, once said: 'The only ingredients that truly matter in barbecuing – beyond the quality of the meat, of course – are smoke and time.' Cooking meat directly or indirectly using fire takes practice, patience and planning.

Barbecues come in a variety of shapes and sizes; from small, portable ones to large kettle- or barrel- shaped ones. All of these are designed for use with solid fuels, of which there are two types: lump charcoal and briquettes. Lump charcoal is made by burning solid wood in a reduced-oxygen atmosphere. This drives off the impurities that cause the smoke you see if you burn ordinary wood. It burns quickly and gets hot fast; after that, though, it cools rapidly. This is great for quickly grilling things like steaks and sausages. For bigger, slower cooked pieces of meat you'll need to top it up.

Charcoal briquettes are the other main type of fuel available. These are made from charcoal dust and coal dust held together with a starch binder. The advantage of these is their uniform shape and the fact that they burn for longer. Because they're made of bits of stuff, they're often a lot cheaper too. They also produce more ash than lump wood. It's horses for courses, but of the two, I prefer proper charcoal. You can also use wood chips to augment the smoky flavour. Finally I'm not really a fan of those disposable barbecues: they're chemical, nasty and barely able to cook a sausage – don't bother.

WAYS OF COOKING

Grilling, as it's known in the USA, is cooking things quickly directly over the coals. This is best for burgers, steaks, fish, kebabs and such things. If you're going to do steaks, bigger, thicker ones work better, allowing for that lovely telltale barbecue crust to form on the outside, without completely overcooking the centre.

Proper barbecuing is cooking things much, much slower, often indirectly. The glowing coals are moved to one side and the radiant heat and smoke do the work. Use this method to cook much larger pieces of meat, as well as tougher meat, such as ribs and brisket. Part of the joy of barbecuing is the vast rubs, sauces and marinade options available. These are the paints to your meat canvas, which add extra flavours, taste and spice. See page 162 for some basic rub recipes.

CHIMNEY STARTERS

These are small metal barrels with holes in the bottom that allow air in and up through the charcoal that you place inside. Just put some newspaper underneath, light it, and 10–20 minutes later the coals are ready. You then just pick up the chimney and tip the coals out into the rest of the barbecue. Using one of these means you don't have to use lighter fluid and other stinky substances that might affect the taste of your cooking.

This is just a bit of a heads-up on the world of barbecuing; it's a huge area with lots of potential for great-tasting meat. If you want to explore it further, there's a Haynes manual for that too.

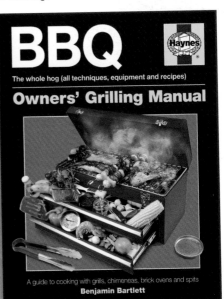

BBQ Haynes

The whole hog (all techniques, equipment and recipes)

Owners' Grilling Manual

A guide to cooking with grills, chimeneas, brick ovens and spits
Benjamin Bartlett

Cooking times

THESE COOKING TIMES ARE APPROXIMATE AND BASED ON A STANDARD FAN-ASSISTED OVEN.

ROAST CHICKEN

Oven temperature – 180°C
25 minutes per 500g, plus an extra 25 minutes
Internal temperature – 73-75°C

ROAST PORK

Loin, leg, shoulder, belly
Oven temperature – 180°C
Medium – 30 mins per 450g + 30 mins
Well done – 35 mins per 450g + 35mins
Internal temperature – 70°C

ROAST BEEF

Sirloin, Topside, Top Rump, Silverside, Rib joint
Oven temperature – 180°C
Rare – 20mins per 450g + 20mins
Medium – 25mins per 450g + 25mins
Well done – 30mins per 450g + 30mins
Internal temperature: rare – 60°C, medium – 70°C,
well done – 80°C

ROAST LAMB

Leg, shoulder, breast
Oven temperature – 180°C
Medium – 25mins per 450g + 25 mins
Well done – 30 mins per 450g + 30 mins
Internal temperature: medium – 70-75°C,
well done – 75-80°C

How to make a cartouche

If you're slow-cooking dishes such as beef stew (page 96), pigs' cheeks (page 77) or hare ragu (page 138) in the oven, then a cartouche is invaluable.

A cartouche is simply a disc of greaseproof paper with a hole in. It does two things: firstly, it stops a crust or skin forming on the casserole and secondly, it stops the liquids evaporating too quickly.

Why not just use the lid the pot came with? Well if you cook a stew with a tight-fitting lid on, the steam can't escape and so ends up back in your casserole, which can make it watery. I have, on occasion, when out of greaseproof paper, unscrewed the handle from the lid of my casserole, which lets the steam out through the remaining hole.

EQUIPMENT
- Greaseproof paper
- Casserole
- Pencil
- Scissors or scalpel

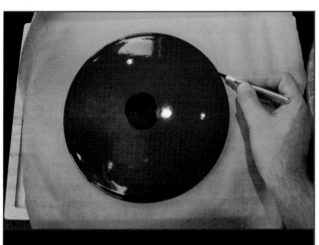

1 Lay a sheet of greaseproof paper on a large chopping board and place your cold, empty casserole on top.

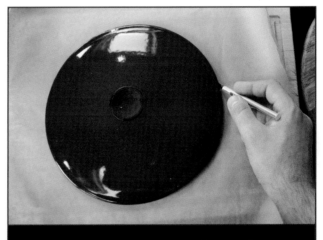

2 Draw roughly around your pan with a pencil.

3 Remove the pan. Cut out the disc, trimming off the pencil line.

4 Snip a little cross in the top of the disc to let out the steam. You can now place your cartouche on your casserole before putting it in the oven.

CHAPTER 2
POULTRY

Taking apart and working with chicken is one of the best ways to improve your knife skills and practise some of the basics of butchery. It's normally cheaper to buy a whole bird and break it down yourself than to buy individual cuts too.

Chickens are cheaper than other meats (this problem is discussed on the next page), and part of their success is that there are so many options and flavours you can marry with them, from spices to pastry to fruit. However, don't forget some of the other poultry available; ducks, guinea fowl and turkeys are delicious too!

The problem with chicken

Of course it's completely apocryphal, but Henry IV of France (1553–1610) – known as 'Good King Henry' for his devotion to the health of his people – is reputed to have said something along the lines of: 'I wish for a chicken in every peasant's pot on Sunday.'

In fact, the quote first appears 50 years after Henry's death in the work of historian Hardouin Péréfixe de Beaumont, but you can see why it might be attractive. There's the symbolism of the Church, the king and the people – and added to which is the cockerel, symbol of France.

'A chicken in every pot' was such a powerful symbol of aspiration and social contentment that it was used again on a Republican Party flyer in 1928. This subsequently got attached to the Republican Presidential candidate, Herbert Hoover, though he never said the phrase either.

So the idea of a chicken on a Sunday still resonates down the centuries, yet there was a time when chicken was a luxury. Speak to anyone who grew up in 1940s and 1950s Britain, and they'll tell you that chicken was for high days and holidays.

The poultry chapter of Nell Heaton's *The Complete Cook* from 1953 starts with how to kill, pluck and gut the bird. I'll spare you

that, but it goes to show how rare and special chicken once was. Sadly, today it's become the generic, white, bland protein of choice – and this is a shame.

You like chicken – right? Of course you do, everyone does. What does it taste of, then? Close your eyes and describe its flavour and aroma. Not that of gravy, or the spicy sauce slathered on it, but the actual taste of proper chicken? Tricky isn't it?

Here's why: the average age at which a standard chicken in the EU is slaughtered is just 42 days. They are bred to gain weight quickly and because they don't have a chance to fully mature they never develop proper flavour. It takes less time for a chicken to go from hatching to slaughter than it does for you to order and take delivery of a new sofa.

Chicken – once thought of as lean, healthy meat – has, like many of us, got fat. A 2009 study at London Metropolitan University found that 45 years ago, chicken had 8g of fat per 100g serving, while today it has more than 22g of fat per serving; that's twice the amount of a portion of ice cream (while the amount of protein has declined by a third).

REAL CHICKEN

There are some excellent producers of chicken in the UK today: Copas in Berkshire produce larger, older chickens, as well as turkeys. Label Anglaise is another well-respected producer, as is Sutton Hoo Chicken, based in Suffolk. The Botterill family in Leicestershire produce amazing hens and cockerels, which are available online or via The Ginger Pig chain of butchers. That's just a handful; there are plenty of others up and down the UK.

Many smaller producers only grow on chickens for the winter market. A real chicken will cost more, but it'll be bigger and older which means a much better flavour. A typical chicken from one of these producers will be 12–18 weeks old, rather than the 4–6 of a factory bird. They're also going to have a much thicker skin, more like a turkey, which will crisp up beautifully.

OTHER BIRDS

Why is it we only eat turkey once a year? Around 10 million are eaten over the festive period. Turkey rather unfairly has a reputation for being dry and bland. Turns out you've been eating the wrong turkey!

Around one million free-range turkeys are produced in Britain: look for breeds such as the Norfolk Black or the Norfolk Bronze. Like proper chickens, a free-range slow-growing bird can cost up to three times as much, but are your family not worth it? This is the centrepiece of the biggest dinner of the year – don't be tight! If you thought intensive chicken farming was bad, it's even worse for ducks. At present, 'there is no duck meat currently available in the UK that can be considered acceptable on welfare grounds', according to the RSPCA. Many producers don't give the ducks access to water to bathe in, which is second nature to a duck. Small-scale and organic producers have higher welfare standards, so try to seek these out. Finally, between September and January you might be able to get your hands on some wild duck; mallard being the most popular.

SPATCHCOCK CHICKEN

A great way of cooking chicken quickly and easily, particularly on a barbecue or under a grill. Spatchcocking is the process of removing the bird's backbone and sternum, which allows the remaining breasts and legs to be flattened out. The reason for flattening the bird like this is that it allows each side of the meat to come into contact with the heat source, ensuring a faster cooking time. You can also hold the bird together with two skewers, which makes turning it over easier.

EQUIPMENT
- Knife or pair of poultry scissors
- Metal or wooden skewers

METHOD
1. Turn the chicken upside down and identify the backbone.
2. Using your knife or a pair of poultry scissors (these do make this easier), cut along one side of the backbone.
3. Turn the bird over and press down firmly on the breast to break the keel bone and flatten the carcass out.
4. Using a metal or wooden skewer, pierce the bird diagonally from drumstick to breast and repeat on the other side.

Brining poultry

Brining is the act of submerging any meat into a saline (i.e. salty) solution. You can brine most meat, but it works particularly well with leaner meats, such as poultry. Brining helps the meat remain juicy when cooked.

To be clear, brining doesn't make the meat taste salty, but instead the salt works on breaking down some of the muscle proteins in the meat, allowing them to soak up the water and retain it during cooking.

WHAT TO BRINE IN

You can brine in anything: a bucket, a large plastic tub, a washing-up bowl. I brined a turkey one Christmas in a large beer-brewing bucket. Whatever you use, just make sure it's spotlessly clean and has not been used for mopping the floor, or suchlike. A deep, square tub with a lid is ideal and stops the water from sloshing about as you move it.

Always brine in the fridge if you can. If that's not possible, use the coolest place you can find, such as a garage or porch. Add some ice cubes or ice packs to keep things really cold; you want to keep the water around 4°C. Never leave the brine in direct sunlight.

TO MAKE A BRINE

Heat up 1 litre of water in a pan and add your total salt content to this. Your brine should be a 5% solution: so use 50g of salt per litre of water. Ordinary table salt will do: I wouldn't use best-quality sea salt for this – it's a waste. Stir to fully dissolve the salt.

As well as the salt, some people add other aromatics to their solutions, such as sugar, juniper berries, bay leaves, all spice berries, cinnamon sticks, peppercorns, lemons, oranges, garlic, sage leaves and rosemary. Unless you're adding a lot, not much of these extra flavours will get into your meat – you're just making homeopathic chicken.

Once done, place in the bucket, top up with the rest of the water and leave to go completely cold. Only then, add your meat. A key ingredient in brining is time: for something like chicken or turkey, leave it at least overnight.

Be careful when removing your bird from the brining tub, as you don't want to drip water everywhere. Hold upside down over the bucket to pour out any water that's collected in the cavity, then transfer to your raw meat board and pat the surface dry with plenty of kitchen paper.

Pour some vegetable oil onto a final piece of kitchen paper. Smear this over the skin and give it a light dusting of salt. This will help the skin crisp up beautifully. That's it; you're ready to roast!

OTHER LIQUIDS

So, not only can you brine using water, you can also start to play around with other liquids. This is nothing new – after all the classic coq au vin sees the chicken brined in wine. Dairy options, meanwhile, include milk and buttermilk, which are both used extensively in the American South. The acid in buttermilk helps to tenderise the meat. Staying in the South, I've even seen recipes that use sweetened ice tea and lemon.

Beer can also be used: floral or citrus beers work really well. You can even go down the cider vinegar route, which will give your chicken a tangy flavour. For other ways to add flavour to your meat, check out the rubs and marinades on page 162.

Removing the wishbone for easy carving

This is one of the most basic pieces of butchery you can do – and yet one that delivers real, helpful results. Removing the wishbone from a chicken, turkey or duck makes carving the breasts off much easier. Not only that, it also frees up a little room in the carcass for stuffing.

EQUIPMENT
■ Small knife

1 Open up the neck hole of the bird and remove any excess skin or fat you find. Don't pull the skin back off the breast too much, as you may tear it.

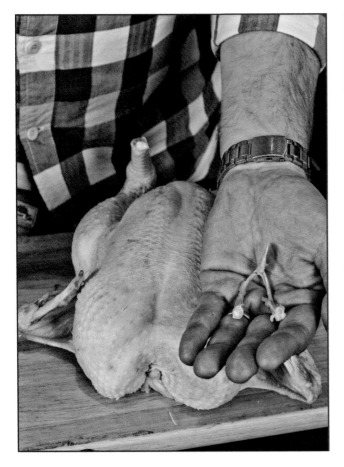

2 Run your fingers down each side of the gap to find the wishbone.
3 Using a small knife, slowly start cutting above and under the length of the wishbone, taking care not to cut the breast meat too much.
4 At the bottom, two bones join the wing area. Work your knife around each bone, gently cutting them free.
5 At the top, the wishbone fuses and joins the cartilage. Again, work your knife slowly around this to cut it free. You may need to twist it a little to remove it.
6 Use your fingers to work the bone free – it may snap. This is okay, as long as you can remove all the pieces of bone.

How to joint a chicken into primal cuts

There are dozens of ways to take apart a chicken, but only one reason why you should – it saves you money. Two fresh skinless, boneless chicken breasts cost not much less than a whole bird.

If you're making chicken Kiev, for example (see page 38), you'll be doing a bit of butchery and prep anyway and it's not that much effort to start with the whole thing. The legs can be frozen and used in everything from a pie to a stir-fry, while the carcass can be used to make stock (see page 169) for enriching soups. Practise on a cheaper bird first if you're unsure.

EQUIPMENT
■ Medium-sized sharp knife

. . . .

1 Remove the wishbone from the bird (see page 29). You don't have to do this, but it'll make carving the breasts off a lot easier.
2 With the bird breast-side down, run your knife around where the leg meets the body through the skin and flesh. Gently pop the thigh bone out of its socket. Repeat for the other leg.
3 Flex the joint where the drumstick meets the thigh to gauge exactly where it is. Run your knife around and down between the joint: I tend to start on the 'inside' of the joint. Remove the drumstick from the thigh. I take the ankles off too.
4 Place the carcass on its back and turn your attention to the breasts. The white, hard bit between them is called the keel bone: you want to cut either side of that. Place the front of the chicken towards you and start at the back, cutting down the breast in one clean movement, just to the left of the centre. Open out the flesh slightly and start to cut away from the rib cage.

5 With the back of the breast removed, come to the front. You'll hit the wishbone unless you've removed it, cut around that and off the carcass to remove the breast.
6 Unless you want the wings for a recipe, I think they're best added to the stock, as they'll help to set it. Alternatively, you can leave them on. If you do want to separate them, turn the carcass over and run your knife around the joint to remove them. The wing tips are definitely for the stockpot.
7 Under the main breast is the mini fillet, which will easily pull away. If you're making a stew or casserole, cut the breast pieces into thirds.

How to carve a whole roast chicken

Sunday lunch, family all round, drop of something nice in a glass and a chicken in the oven – that's the perfect Sunday in my book. Carving a roast chicken is a very similar method to jointing a raw one. You want to end up with two drumsticks, two thighs, two wings and two breasts sliced into four or five thick slices. This should – depending on appetites around the table – feed six people. Although, if growing teenage boys are present, revise that number down.

Here's how I carve chicken breasts: instead of slicing meat front to back off the breast, remove the whole thing (which is easy, because you've already taken out the wishbone – right?) and slice each breast from top to bottom. That way, everyone gets a piece of meat that ranges from the deliciously crispy skin, right down to where the meat meets the rib cage.

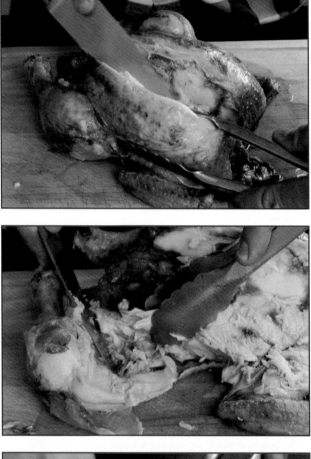

EQUIPMENT
- Tongs or a carving fork
- Large chopping board or carving board
- Cook's knife or carving knife
- Large, warm serving plate

1 Let the chicken rest for 15–20 minutes before attempting to carve. This relaxes the meat and makes carving easier.
2 Using a pair of tongs or a carving fork, secure the bird on a chopping board or carving board and insert your knife to the left of the central (or keel) bone. Cut down to remove the left breast and set aside. Repeat on the other side to remove the right breast and set aside.
3 Remove the legs by popping out the thigh bone. Place your knife on the drumstick joint and cut to separate the drumstick from the thigh.
4 With your tongs, slice each breast laterally (as in top to bottom) into 4–6 thick slices. You may want to remove the mini fillet (the smaller piece that sits under the main breast meat) and serve whole.
5 Arrange sliced breast meat, thighs and drumsticks on your warm serving plate. Any juices that have run onto your board can be poured over. Save the now stripped-bare carcass for stock.

Classic roast chicken

Along with making a Victoria sponge, being able to roast a chicken competently is something anyone who considers themselves interested in cooking should be able to do. Some shops have tried to make the process foolproof with foil trays, rubs and roasting bags, but I think you can't beat doing it the proper way. There are a few tips and tricks that take your birds from bog-standard to brilliant. You don't have to do all these on the one bird!

INGREDIENTS

- 1 free-range large chicken
- 2 carrots
- 2 onions
- 2 sticks of celery
- 1 tablespoon of vegetable oil
- Sprinkle of salt

TIPS FOR ROASTING CHICKEN

- Take your chicken out of the fridge 45 minutes before you want to cook it – *do not* wash it. Dry the skin with kitchen paper. Use a pastry brush to apply a thin layer of oil over the skin and then sprinkle over some salt.
- Start your bird off breast-side down: this lets all the fat from the bird drain down through the breasts, which helps keep them moist. It also allows the skin on the underside to get going. Turn back over halfway through cooking to brown the breasts, and give them a sprinkle of salt.
- Most standard store-brought chickens contain quite a lot of fat. You don't want the underside of your bird swimming around in that, so buy a roasting tin with a rack, or make a trivet from lots of vegetables to raise the bird up. This will speed up the cooking process and help the skin underneath crisp. Or buy a better-quality chicken.

- Remove the wishbone for easy carving. This is discussed in more detail on page 29.
- Brine the chicken (see page 28), add a dry rub (page 162) or stuff some herb butter (page 163) under the skin. You can also fill the cavity with half a lemon, garlic cloves or more herbs.
- I don't add pepper to the surface of a bird prior to roasting, as I think it can burn, giving a bitter taste. It's better to add it at the end.
- Starting the bird off at a high temperature before turning the oven down helps to ensure crispy skin. However, if you're slow-roasting a large bird, you can do it at the end.
- After cooking the chicken, let it rest for at least 15 minutes. Up to 30 minutes is good, as long as it's somewhere warm.
- Don't smother the chicken in foil when it's resting, it'll just sweat.

1. Remove the chicken from the fridge. Preheat the oven to 200ºC.
2. Roughly chop the carrots, onions and celery and add to the roasting tray with a glug of oil.
3. Portion out the vegetable oil and salt into separate saucers or cups. You don't want to be picking up the salt grinder or oil bottle with 'raw chicken hands'.
4. Pour over the oil and massage all over the bird's skin, or use a pastry brush. Sprinkle over the salt and ensure it's rubbed all over.
5. Place the chicken breast-side-down on the rack or trivet of vegetables.
6. Place in the oven for 20 minutes before lowering the temperature to 170ºC and turning over the chicken, so the breasts face upwards. How long your chicken takes to cook will depend on its size. Most commercial chickens are around the 1.5–2kg mark – I find these usually take about an hour, but check the packaging for an exact cooking time.
7. Leave the chicken to rest somewhere warm for 15 minutes (or longer) before carving. This will give you time to make the gravy.

IS IT DONE?

'Until the juice runs clear' goes the oft-repeated mantra for cooking chicken. Now that may have been fine in the olden days, but it's not very scientific. Use your £4 meat thermometer and stick it into the breast and thigh. Take a reading: you want an internal temperature of 73–75ºC.

Chicken casserole

A highly versatile dish, the chicken casserole can be tweaked in all manner of ways. You can make it from leftover roast chicken or with fresh chicken pieces. I'm using thighs, as they're cheaper and have more flavour – allow two per person – but you can, of course, swap for breast meat.

You can tweak the vegetables you add, depending on what's in season: asparagus tips in May, parsnips in November. Tarragon is optional, but it does go great with chicken: replace with parsley if you like. The same goes for the mustard: if you don't like it, leave it out. You can even swap the wine for cider (I did say it was versatile). Finally, I like my casserole to have a good amount of flavourful sauce that I can soak up with bread, mash or even rice, which is why my recipe doesn't include potatoes in the casserole itself.

INGREDIENTS

Serves 4

- 8 chicken thighs (or a combination of thighs and drumsticks) or around 400g leftover cooked chicken meat
- 2 onions
- 1 garlic clove, crushed, or cube of frozen garlic
- 1 stick of celery
- 2 medium-sized carrots
- Handful of frozen peas
- 100ml white wine (or cider)
- 50g butter
- 45g flour
- 100ml chicken stock
- Chopped tarragon (or a pinch of dried; won't have quite the same flavour, though)

1. Cut the onions and celery into thin slices and the carrots into batons. Get your peas and other ingredients portioned out and ready.

2. In a casserole or large sauté pan, brown the thighs skin-side-down, two-at-a-time until the skin is golden, then remove and set aside on kitchen paper. (The chicken isn't yet cooked – you've just browned the surface.)

3. Add the onions, garlic, celery and carrots to the pan and cook in the fat left by the chicken. Add a splash of white wine to loosen them if they need it.

4. When the vegetables have coloured and softened a little, remove them and place them with the chicken.

5. Add the butter to the pan. When melted, add the flour and mix together to make a roux. When all the flour is absorbed, add the white wine and stock to make your sauce. Bring up to a simmer and then add the chicken pieces and vegetables back into the pan.

6. You can now leave the casserole to cook on a low heat on the hob for 30 minutes (technically this makes it a stew), or place it in the oven at 160ºC for the same amount of time.

7. Add the peas and chopped tarragon 10 minutes before the casserole is ready.

8. Serve on a plate with mash and green beans, or in a bowl with chunks of fresh bread and butter.

Poached chicken

During the summer months when it's too hot to roast, poached chicken comes into its own. It's quicker than roasting and leaves you halfway to having a stunning stock, as well as juicy leftovers. A poached chicken needs nothing more than a good salad, some homemade mayo or caper sauce, crusty bread and a crisp white wine.

INGREDIENTS

Serves 4

- 1 large free-range chicken
- 2 carrots, topped and tailed
- 2 sticks of celery, washed
- 2 onions, peeled with the root still on and quartered
- 1 lemon, halved
- A few whole peppercorns
- 1 bay leaf (optional)
- 1 fennel bulb, quartered
- A few sprigs of parsley and thyme
- Salt and pepper, to season

RAVIGOTE SALAD

Assemble the salad from whichever leaves you like: round lettuce, watercress, chicory or little gem would all be fine. This is my tweaked version of the classic French sauce, ravigote. It should be punchy ('ravigote' means 'rejuvenated').

INGREDIENTS

- 2 tablespoons of capers, chopped
- 2 tablespoons of baby gherkins, chopped
- 1 tablespoon of parsley, chopped
- 1 tablespoon of tarragon, chopped (or a big pinch, if dried)
- 1 garlic clove, grated
- Good glug of olive oil
- Salt and pepper, to season

Chop everything as finely as you can be bothered, or blitz using a blender.

METHOD

1 You'll need a very large stockpot, big enough to hold the chicken fully submerged in the water. Place the bird in the pot and add all the other ingredients around it. Place on the stove and fill slowly with water by repeatedly using a measuring jug. This helps prevent splashes from the raw chicken from covering your sink and draining board.

2 Make sure you leave about 8–10cm between the waterline and the top of the pan.

3 Turn on the heat and bring it up to a rolling boil, then turn down to a gentle simmer.

Poach the chicken for an hour, then turn out the heat and leave it somewhere to cool in the stock for about 30 minutes (if you remove it now, it'll dry out and go a bit tough). Poached chicken should be served juicy and warm, not hot.

4 When the chicken has cooled, remove it from the water (be careful, as the cavity will be full of water).

5 Carve it into primal cuts (see page 30), further slice the breasts and place the meat on a warmed plate. The benefit of poaching is that you get wonderfully moist meat, but at the expense of crispy skin, so I recommend that you don't serve the skin.

6 Serve with the salad (see panel), sauce, bread and wine. The carcass and any bones can go back in the poaching liquor along with fresh carrots, onions and celery, and placed on a simmer to make stock (see page 169).

Fried chicken

If you spot free-range chicken thighs and drumsticks on offer, snaffle them up and make this Southern USA-inspired classic. Like Scotch eggs (page 70) or arancini, it's best made in a deep fat fryer.

INGREDIENTS

Serves 8–10

For the buttermilk marinade:
- 1 carton of buttermilk
- 2 tablespoons of Worcestershire sauce
- 2 tablespoons of Tabasco sauce
- Salt and pepper, to season

For the coating:
- 10–12 chicken drumsticks or thighs
- 300g plain flour
- 2 teaspoons of cayenne pepper
- 2 teaspoons of mustard powder
- 2 teaspoons of paprika
- Salt and pepper, to season
- 3 litres vegetable oil

I've marinated the meat in buttermilk, but you can skip this step if you're in a hurry and just coat the chicken in beaten egg. I actually use a special plastic tub that attaches to my vacuum sealer and marinades the meat under a vacuum, which speeds things up no end.

METHOD

1 Mix together the buttermilk marinade ingredients and add the chicken. Combine so the meat is completely covered and leave in the fridge for a minimum of 4 hours, or ideally overnight.

2 Mix the flour with the cayenne pepper, mustard powder, paprika, salt and pepper. Wipe off most of the buttermilk mixture from the chicken pieces and toss them in the flavoured flour until the chicken is fully coated. Set aside. I recommend repeating this step, particularly with your first pieces, just to make sure the chicken is fully coated.

3 When you're ready to cook the chicken, heat the vegetable oil in your deep fat fryer to 170°C (or use a large high-sided saucepan, filled no more than halfway up). Heat the oven to 100°C so you can keep the cooked pieces warm and place in a roasting tray with a wire rack.

4 Add the chicken pieces, two at a time, to the oil and cook for about 10–15 minutes, until golden brown.

5 When cooked, transfer the chicken pieces to the heated roasting tray in the oven to drain and keep warm while you get on with the next batch.

6 Serve with homemade 'slaw, fries and beer.

Jerk chicken

This recipe comes from my friend, the food writer and self-confessed jerk junky, Helen Graves. South London is one of the best places to get jerk in the UK, although considering the long relationship Britain has had with the Caribbean its food isn't as popular as that of other cuisines, which is a shame. Jerk, then, is more a homely thing – a family thing.

INGREDIENTS

Serves 4–6

- 4–6 chicken legs (or other chicken pieces of an equivalent size)
- 55g dark brown packed (muscovado) sugar
- 4 garlic cloves, peeled
- 1 tablespoon of fresh thyme leaves
- 1 bunch of large spring onions (about 5)
- 1½ tablespoons of allspice berries, ground
- ½ teaspoon of ground cinnamon
- ¼ teaspoon of ground nutmeg
- ½ teaspoon of ground ginger
- ½ teaspoon of ground cloves
- 3 fresh Scotch bonnet chillies, seeded
- Slug of dark rum
- Juice of 2 limes
- 1 teaspoon of salt
- Black pepper, to taste

There are two styles of jerk: either a dry rub, in which all the dry ingredients are rubbed over the raw meat, or a marinade, in which the meat is submerged in a sauce of wet ingredients for many hours. This is the latter. It's also cooked indirectly over charcoal, which adds to the smoky flavour. If you're not firing up the grill, you can cook it in the oven for around 30 minutes at 180ºC, but it's not quite the same, though.

METHOD

1 To make the marinade for the jerk chicken put all the ingredients, except the chicken, in a blender and whizz together until smooth. Smother the marinade over the chicken legs, rubbing it in well.

2 Refrigerate for at least 4 hours or overnight.

3 Allow the meat to come to room temperature and brush off most of the excess marinade before grilling it on the barbecue. To set up your barbecue for the indirect cooking method, light the coals in the middle in a kind of volcano shape. Wait for the flames to disappear, leaving you with coals that have a light grey ash coating. Move them to the sides. This gets the indirect heat circulating around the kettle when you put the lid on. You should also brush the grate with a little oil.

4 The chicken pieces will take about 30 minutes to cook (although it depends on size) – always check with your meat thermometer before serving.

A proper chicken Kiev

The origins of this dish are much disputed – is it Russian, French or Ukrainian? You'll find people prepared to take all sides. What is certain is that it was the first prepared, chilled ready-meal Marks & Spencer sold in the UK in 1976. For a time it even appeared on restaurant menus, along with that other 1970s Russian dish you rarely see anymore, beef stroganoff.

So, time to bring it back, I say. It's another recipe that tests your chicken filleting skills. A note on the garlic: most garlic in shops these days is inferior stuff, mainly from China, with little punch or bite. If it's got that green core, it may be up to a year old. So for dishes like this, I use frozen cubes of pureed garlic, which you can find in the freezer section. You can also find it as a paste in tubes. It's far less hassle than pounding garlic in a pestle, but if you want to do that, go ahead.

. . . .

INGREDIENTS
Serves 2
- Small bunch of parsley and tarragon, finely chopped
- 30g butter, at room temperature
- 1 cube of defrosted frozen garlic, or a large squeeze from a tube
- 2 free-range chicken breasts, removed from a whole chicken (save the legs for something else), or two pre-bought chicken breasts
- 2 free-range eggs
- 3 tablespoons of flour
- 70g panko breadcrumbs
- 2.5 litres vegetable oil, if frying

METHOD
1 First, make the filling. In a bowl, combine the herbs, butter and garlic. Transfer to a piece of cling film and roll into a sausage shape. Place in the freezer to set firm.
2 Remove the wishbone from the bird and then take off the breasts from either side. Remove the legs and freeze for another dish, and keep the rib cage for stock. Remove the skin from the breast meat, and also the mini fillet, found under the main breast.
3 Using a small knife, make a 2cm incision at the thickest end of the breast. Poke your finger in and wiggle it about from side to side to make a small pocket, trying not to make the entrance hole any bigger.
4 Take your now-firmed-up butter sausage shape from the freezer and push into the hole you've just made, pinching the entrance closed as best you can. Don't overload it: you may not need all the butter.
5 Secure the entry hole with a cocktail stick and place the breast in the fridge for an hour, again to firm up.
6 Clean down your bench and get the egg, flour and breadcrumbs ready in three separate shallow bowls. Add 1 tablespoon of flour to the breadcrumbs and stir in thoroughly.
7 Take the chicken breasts out of the fridge, remove the cocktail stick and roll them in the flour, then the egg and then the breadcrumb / flour mix.
8 Heat the oven to 150°C and heat the vegetable oil in a deep fat fryer or saucepan to 160°C.
   Gently place one fillet in the oil and cook for just under 10 minutes. Transfer to a plate lined with kitchen paper and place in the oven to finish cooking and keep warm while you cook the next one.
9 Both Kievs can be kept in the oven for another 20 minutes while you get any side dishes ready. Chips are sort of traditional, but again that's another fried thing, which might make things a little greasy. I'd opt for some good green veggies, and if you do want carbs, go for mash or even a good ol' jacket spud.

Buffalo wings

Invented in Buffalo, New York, in the late 1960s, these hot and spicy chicken wings have now become to US sporting events what strawberries are to Wimbledon or a pre-match pie is to football. Easy to make, you can eat them with one hand, leaving the other free to hold a beer.

INGREDIENTS

Serves 6–10

For the buffalo wings:
- A dozen free-range chicken wings
- 70g butter
- 1 bottle (about 150ml) of hot spicy sauce
- 2.5 litres vegetable or sunflower oil for deep frying

For the blue cheese dip:
- 100g soft blue cheese, crumbled
- 3 tablespoons of mayonnaise
- 3 tablespoons of sour cream
- 1 tablespoon of white wine or cider vinegar
- Salt and pepper

METHOD

1 Take the wings out of the fridge 20 minutes before cooking.
2 Make the blue cheese dip by blitzing all the ingredients in a food processor or mashing them together in a bowl with a fork.
3 Next make the hot sauce. Melt the butter in a pan and then add the hot spicy sauce. Combine and set aside.
4 Heat the oven to 100ºC and heat your oil in a saucepan or deep fat fryer to 180ºC. Place a wire rack over a baking tray lined with kitchen paper and place in the oven.
5 Add a few wings to the oil at a time and cook for 8–10 minutes, before transferring them to the rack in the oven to keep warm.
6 When all the wings are cooked, slather over the hot sauce and leave them to cool a little. Serve with the blue cheese dip and beers.

Please get good chicken to make these. If you're using wings from a bird that's never had the space to flap them, there's not going to be much meat on there; just skin, bone and gristle. Even free-range wings won't break the bank. If you're after a lot, you might want to let your butcher know a few days in advance, so he can start saving them up from the carcasses he's breaking down.

In the US, Frank's hot sauce is traditionally used, combined with butter. It is available over here now, but any hot spicy sauce is fair game. The accompanying dip is blue cheese – a doddle to make.

OTHER OPTIONS

- You can dip the wings in buttermilk and coat them in breadcrumbs, if you like.
- If you don't fancy deep-frying the wings, you can bake them on the wire rack in the oven.

'Parmo' from Middlesbrough

Just as Milan has its veal Milanese, Teesside has 'Parmo' (short for chicken Parmesan). If you're not from 'The Boro' or surrounding area, you've probably never heard of it. It consists of a flattened chicken breast coated in breadcrumbs and fried, topped with béchamel sauce and grated cheddar cheese – not Parmesan. Follow @ParmoHunters on Twitter for the guide to the best Parmos in the region.

If you replace the traditional accompaniment of chips with rice and the béchamel and cheese with curry sauce, it's the Japanese dish of 'chicken katsu' (see page 76). This goes to prove that breadcrumbed chicken breast with sauce and some form of carbs is a universal human truth. Here then, is my take on this North Eastern classic.

A whole chicken costs not much more than two skinless chicken breast fillets, so buy a whole bird, remove the breasts and skin them. (Save the legs for something else and the carcass for stock.)

Photo © Parmo Hunters

INGREDIENTS
Serves 2
For the chicken in breadcrumbs:
- 2 free-range, skinless chicken breasts
- 2 large eggs
- 1 pack of panko breadcrumbs
- 1 tablespoon of plain flour on a plate
- 2 litres vegetable oil for frying

For the béchamel topping:
- 50g butter
- 45g flour
- 300ml milk
- 100g grated cheddar cheese

METHOD

1 First, make the béchamel. Melt the butter in a saucepan over a low heat until runny. Add the flour, which will foam up. Stir the mixture vigorously with a wooden spoon. It will clump together, but keep stirring – you want to cook the flour in the butter. When it's settled down a bit and returned to a more liquid state, add cold milk a little at a time. It will immediately turn solid again: just keep gently stirring. As the sauce combines you may want to switch to using a whisk. When fully incorporated take off the heat, cover the saucepan with cling film to stop a skin forming and set aside.

2 Fill a large pan for frying no more than two-thirds full with the oil and heat to 170ºC. Heat the grill to around 150ºC.

3 Beat the eggs together and tip onto a large plate next to the plate of flour. Tip the breadcrumbs out onto a third plate.

4 Place the two breasts between two large pieces of cling film on a chopping board and smack with a rolling pin to flatten them.

5 Dredge a chicken breast in the flour, then the egg and then the breadcrumbs. Repeat for the second chicken breast.

6 When the oil's hot, add the chicken breasts and cook for about 10–15 minutes until the crumbs turn golden. Remove and drain on kitchen paper. Repeat for the second 'Parmo'.

7 If you're serving with the traditional chips and salad, now's the time to deep fry them too (the chips that is, not the salad!).

8 Once both 'Parmos' are cooked, place on the grill tray and spread the cooled béchamel sauce over the top of each. Sprinkle over the grated cheddar cheese and place under the grill until the cheese melts and bubbles. Serve immediately for a taste of the North East.

Tandoori chicken legs

Bit cheeky, this, calling these 'tandoori' when neither you (nor I) have an actual tandoori oven! Those clay ovens reach temperatures of over 450°C. To see a naan made in one – the dough stuck to the sides and cooked instantly without falling off and into the coals – is a thing of beauty. What these are really are Indian-style curried chicken legs.

If you really love South-East Asian food, tandoori ovens are available to buy for under £200, or search online for instructions on how to make one from things you can buy at a DIY centre. Also, if you've got an old coffee grinder you want to put out to pasture, grinding the dry spices from whole is a worthy retirement.

I've an excellent cookbook from 1961, entitled *Mrs Balbir Singh's Indian Cookery*, (she was the Delia Smith of Indian cooking back in the day), in which Singh declares 'tandoori murgha' (tandoori chicken) 'the showpiece of the Indian culinary art…the method of preparation is perhaps as ancient as civilisation itself.

INGREDIENTS
Serves 4
- 4 cloves of garlic and 1 thumb-sized piece of fresh ginger *or* 1 cube of frozen garlic and ginger
- 1 tablespoon of ground coriander
- 1 tablespoon of ground cumin
- 1 teaspoon of curry powder
- 1 teaspoon of turmeric
- 1 teaspoon of chilli powder
- 4 tablespoons of natural yoghurt
- 1 teaspoon of vegetable oil
- 4 free-range chicken legs
- Juice of one lime
- Salt and pepper, to season

METHOD
1 Blitz the garlic and ginger in a mini food processor, or reduce to a puree by hand in a pestle and mortar.
2 Toast the dry spices in a warm, dry frying pan to release their flavour.
3 In a bowl large enough to hold the chicken legs, add both the blitzed paste and the spices to the yoghurt and vegetable oil, and combine.
4 Make deep slashes into the meat of the chicken legs, both on the thigh and the drumstick and add to the bowl containing the marinade.
5 Stir well with a spoon, or get your hands in there, so all the chicken is coated in the sauce. Refrigerate for 2 hours, or even overnight.
6 When you're ready to cook the chicken legs, heat your oven to 200°C.
7 Lift each chicken leg or drumstick out of the marinade and shake off any excess. Place on a wire rack above a tray, to catch any drips, and roast in the hot oven for 35 minutes, turning a few times. Check the meat is cooked using a meat thermometer.
8 Squeeze over a little lime juice once cooked, and serve with thinly sliced raw onions, soaked in water to remove their bite, chillies, coriander and a dollop of mango chutney.

Chicken and mushroom pot pie

An absolute classic combination that has stood the test of time (it's even a Pot Noodle flavour). These two ingredients just work so well together.

INGREDIENTS
Serves 6

For the filling:
- 1 tablespoon of vegetable oil
- 10g butter
- 1 large onion, chopped
- 2 cloves of garlic, crushed
- 300g mixed mushrooms
- 250ml chicken stock
- 1 teaspoon of thyme leaves
- 1 small glass of white wine
- Salt and pepper, to season
- 600g cooked chicken meat (roughly about half a leftover chicken)
- 2 tablespoons of crème fraîche

For the pastry:
- 500g ready-made puff pastry (I think this filling suits a puff-topped pot pie, but it would work equally well in a double-lined shortcrust pie)
- 1 beaten egg
- Splash of milk

The key with any use of mushrooms in cooking is to use a variety: that way you get a different taste, shape and texture. White button mushrooms are the pawns of the mushroom world, they're only really good for bulking out filling. Chestnut mushrooms offer a little more flavour. On top of that, you should consider a large portobello or two. Finally, break out the big guns flavour-wise by rehydrating some porcini mushrooms.

METHOD

1 Melt the oil and butter in a pan and gently cook the onion until soft.
2 Add the garlic and mushrooms and cook for about 10 minutes until they begin to soften and take on a little colour. Add the chicken stock, thyme and white wine, and stir. Season with salt and pepper.
3 Add the cooked chicken and the crème fraîche. Leave on a low simmer for 15–20 minutes until well combined and the sauce has thickened. Leave to cool. When cool, transfer to a large pie tin or dish with a pie bird in the centre. Heat the oven to 200ºC.
4 Roll out the pastry to cover your tin (you may need two packets depending on how big your dish is).
5 Make the egg wash by combining the beaten egg with a tiny splash of milk. Brush the edge of the dish with the egg wash, and gently unfurl the pastry from your rolling pin over the dish. Poke through the pie bird and secure. Brush the surface of the pastry with the remaining egg wash until covered. Place in the hot oven for 25–30 minutes until the pastry has risen and is golden brown.

The dish was created by Rosemary Hume and Constance Spry, and called for the chicken to be first poached then left to cool, before being removed from the carcass and shredded into bite-sized pieces. It was then mixed with a creamy curry-flavoured sauce. The dish was served cold, with rice flecked with peas, cucumber and herbs, and mixed with a French dressing. Very summery, though this being an important occasion, the British weather obviously ruined it and it was actually rather cold and grey on that particular June day.

For my version I'm starting with a whole poached chicken, just like the original recipe, but I've upped the heat element with fresh chilli and added a few supporting flavours, such as fresh coriander, which wouldn't have been available in post-war Blightly. This is a great dish to make with leftover chicken too.

INGREDIENTS
Serves 4–8
- 1 whole chicken
- 2 carrots
- 2 sticks of celery
- 2 onions
- A few peppercorns

For the sauce:
- Handful of sliced almonds
- 2 tablespoons of curry powder
- 2 tablespoons of mango chutney
- 250ml Greek yoghurt
- 250ml mayonnaise
- ½ a bunch of coriander
- 1 large red chilli, deseeded and sliced

METHOD
1 Put the chicken in a large pot with the root vegetables and peppercorns, and cover with cold water. Place on the hob and bring up to a boil, removing any scum or bubbles that float to the top. Then turn the heat down and poach gently for about 1 hour. Leave to cool in the water.
2 When cold, remove the bird and with clean hands, shred the meat from the carcass into bite-sized pieces. Reserve in the fridge (this can all be done the day before).
3 To make the sauce, toast the almonds in a dry frying pan and set aside. Using the same still-warm pan, but with the heat off, toast the curry powder to release some of its flavours.
4 Place the powder in a large bowl with the mango chutney and mix in the yoghurt and the mayonnaise. Add the chicken pieces and fully combine.
5 When you are ready to serve, mix through the chopped coriander and sliced chilli, and top with the toasted almonds. Serve with rice or naan.

Coronation chicken

In post-war 1950s Britain, chicken was still something of a luxury (meat remained on ration until 1954). It was therefore considered a fitting dish to serve at the Coronation of a new Queen in 1953, where guests sat down in the Great Hall at Westminster School to Coronation chicken.

Roast duck with bacon and peas

Duck is incredibly versatile; you can roast, fry, smoke and confit it. Not only that, it can take on a huge range of additional flavours. However, it does need careful cooking, as you can dry it out. Another thing to bear in mind with a duck is that you get much less meat on it than you do a chicken: both the drumsticks and breasts are smaller.

The most common duck breed in Britain is the Pekin. Some say it lacks the flavour of an Aylesbury duck, which are better, but harder to find these days. Barbary is another popular variety.

INGREDIENTS

Serves 2 hungry people or 4 people who are being polite
- 2kg whole duck
- Salt and pepper

For the peas:
- 100g unsmoked lardons
- 1 finely diced small onion or shallot
- 1 garlic clove, crushed
- 100ml stock
- 200g frozen peas
- Few leaves of little gem lettuce
- Few sprigs of mint

METHOD

1 To get a good crispy skin on your duck, the night before you are going to eat it remove the packaging, prick the skin all over with the tip of a sharp knife or fork and dust with a little fine table salt.

2 Heat the oven to 200ºC. Place the bird breast-side-up on a wire rack above a deep roasting tray and roast for 25–30 minutes.

3 Remove the tray and pour off the fat that has come out into a cup.

4 Turn the heat down to 180ºC, turn the bird breast-side-down and cook for another 30 minutes, before pouring off the fat once more. Leave somewhere warm to rest while you make the peas.

5 To make the peas, first add the bacon to a pan with a little of the duck fat and cook until lightly brown. Lower the heat and add the onion. After a few minutes, add the garlic and cook until both are soft. Then add the stock and the peas, and cook for a further 5 minutes.

6 When the peas are just cooked add the lettuce and mint; you just want these to wilt in the heat of the peas.

7 Take the breasts off the duck and thinly slice, or serve the legs.

8 Serve in warmed bowls with the peas on the bottom and slices of the duck on top. A dollop of redcurrant jelly wouldn't go amiss too.

Confit duck

Confit duck is one of those techniques born out of the need to preserve food through the winter. Unlike salting, smoking or air-drying, however, confit sees the meat slowly cooked in fat then left to cool. The fat forms an air-tight, waterless atmosphere, which preserves the duck for weeks, even months.

This is a great dish to make if you happen to spot duck legs on special offer. Just grab some aromatics and two cans of duck fat, clear a Saturday afternoon in the diary and get 'comfy' in the kitchen.

INGREDIENTS

- 6 duck legs
- 1 bulb of garlic, separated into cloves, peeled and smashed
- Sprigs of thyme
- Salt
- 2 cans of duck fat

TO USE THE DUCK LEGS

The meat remains stunningly tender, and can be exhumed from the fat, wiped down and given a quick flash fry to create a crispy, yet tender meal. Different regions of France pair confit duck with different side dishes, such as white beans, braised cabbage, mushrooms and fried potatoes. Aside from these classical pairings, confit duck also works well with Asian spicing.

METHOD

1 Sprinkle salt onto the bottom of a high-sided baking tray or ceramic dish. Place the raw duck legs in the dish, skin-side-up and scatter over the garlic, thyme and more salt. Place in the fridge overnight (or for up to two days).

2 Remove the duck legs from the fridge. Wipe off any remaining salt with kitchen paper and place back in the dish.

3 Melt the duck fat in a large saucepan and pour over the duck legs. You want them all in a single layer and fully submerged.

4 Heat the oven to 150°C and place the duck legs inside. Cook for 3–4 hours until the duck legs are tender and can easily be skewered with your meat probe.

5 Carefully lift out your tray and think about the container you're going to keep your duck in: a sturdy plastic container with a lid about the same size as your original baking tray is ideal. It must be scrupulously clean and bone dry. Traditionally, it would have been a simple earthenware pot.

6 Using a fish slice, lift out each leg and transfer it to the plastic container. Pour the fat over the duck legs until they're completely covered once more. Leave to cool and then store in the fridge – or if it's cold and dry enough, a cellar.

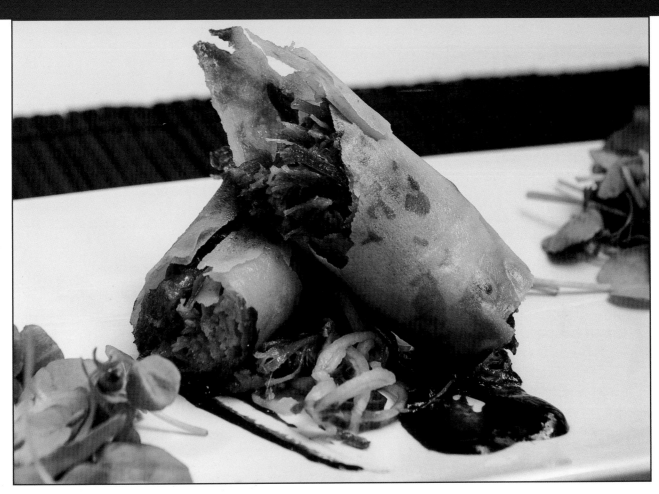

Confit duck parcels

If you shred your confit duck meat it makes a great filling in everything from savoury pancakes to crispy duck parcels. Soy sauce and spring onion would be good accompaniments to these parcels, as would a quick cucumber pickle, which can be made in advance and kept in the fridge.

INGREDIENTS

Serves 2–4

For the duck parcels:

- 2 confit duck legs (see facing page)
- 2 tablespoons of Chinese barbecue or char siu sauce
- 2 tablespoons of melted butter
- 1 packet of filo pastry

For the cucumber pickle:

- ½ cucumber
- 1 teaspoon of sea salt
- 2 tablespoons of rice wine (or white wine) vinegar
- 1 tablespoon of caster sugar

METHOD

1 To make the duck parcels, remove the skin from the cold confit duck and shred the meat from the bone. Mix the meat with the sauce, just to coat it.

2 Melt the butter in a microwave or a pan. Heat the oven to 180°C.

3 Roll out the filo pastry and cut each sheet to 15cm square.

4 Lay a filo pastry sheet on your board, brush with the melted butter then place another on top of that. Repeat until you have four layers.

5 Place the duck meat in the centre, gather up the four corners tightly and pinch together to seal.

6 Place the parcels on a lightly oiled baking tray and bake until golden brown.

7 To make the cucumber pickle, slice the cucumber very finely at an angle. Place it in a colander over the sink and sprinkle over the salt. Place a saucer or small bowl on it and weigh it down with a can or other weight for 20 minutes to extract some of the water. Rinse off any remaining salt and mix the cucumber with the vinegar and sugar.

CHAPTER 3
PORK

As omnivores, pigs are highly efficient at converting human food waste – everything from vegetable scraps to whey leftover from cheese making – into new protein (themselves). Consequently, they've come in for a bit of stick historically, as dirty, messy, lazy animals. Shakespeare himself says 'oh monstrous beast, how like a swine he lies' to describe a drunk tramp in *The Taming of the Shrew*.

There's a 17th-century drawing of a pig by Rembrandt in the British Museum; lean, angry and covered in fur – it looks more like a dog than a pig. Then the Victorians came along and bred out all this wildness to give us nice plump porkers. Today, most people don't see pigs in day-to-day life, whereas just a few generations ago the family pig was the poor household's insurance against the colds of winter.

Which is all a little unfair, as there's great eating on a pig. Everything but the squeak goes the saying, and it's true, you can even eat the tail. Finally, it is the humble pig that gives us bacon – a substance known to improve pretty much everything.

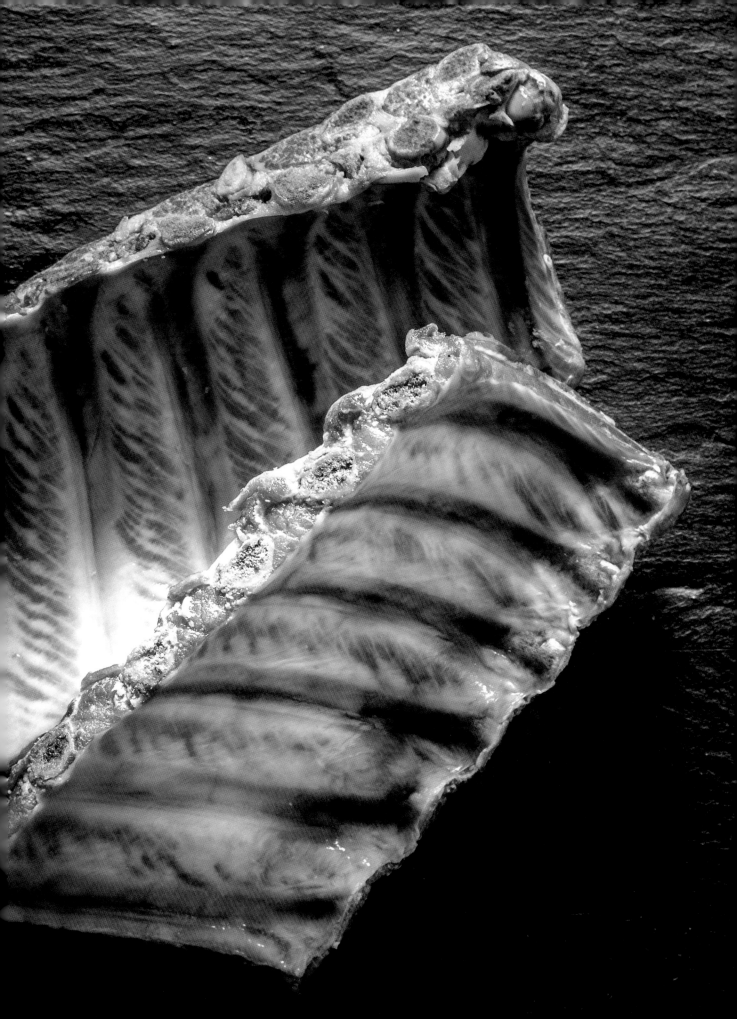

Types of pigs found in the UK

Nearly every county in England once had its own breed of pig; Wales, meanwhile, had the Welsh. Scotland didn't have much of a tradition of pig farming, with the climate and terrain suiting beef production instead. Each pig breed was the result of different needs, uses and environments. Those with longer backs were used to make bacon; large rear legs made the best hams.

Today the most popular pig breeds are often specialised crossbreeds (or breeding pyramids) of Duroc, Landrace and/ or Large White. This is because the resulting animals have the right size and shape, as well as the all-important leanness that many consumers and supermarkets demand. There's also the consistency in litter (the name for a batch of piglets) size to factor in, as well as ease of keeping and how fast they grow. At the other end of the scale are traditional or heritage breeds.

SOME POPULAR PIG BREEDS

DUROC

Duroc
A red-coated pig developed on the East Coast of America in the 1800s and today used in many crossbreeding programmes. Meat from Duroc pigs tends to look a little darker and redder than that from other breeds.

The British Landrace
First imported into Britain from Sweden in 1949, it is now one of the most popular breeds in the country. One of its chief assets is its ability to improve other breeds when crossed with them.

Middle White
Originating in Yorkshire and so called because it fell between the Small White and Large White pigs (the former now extinct), this breed was popular in Victorian times and was known in the capital as 'the London Porker'. Medium-sized in build, it has a slightly 'dished' face (a squashed, slightly upturned snout).

GLOUCESTER OLD SPOT

Gloucester Old Spot Pigs
Poster boy for the rare breed pork movement, this pig was traditionally found in the western county's many orchards pigging out on fallen apples. The spots on its back are said to have been where apples landed.

Tamworth
Hairy, hardy and ginger, and native to the Midlands. This breed was unfashionable in Victorian times and so wasn't put into an improvement crossbreeding programme like many others.

TAMWORTH

BERKSHIRE

THE DEMISE AND RISE OF TRADITIONAL BREEDS

In 1954, there were only 163 registered Tamworth sows and 72 boars. A Government report the next year advised: 'The pig industry will in our view only make real progress when it concentrates on a few main types [or] single type of pig for commercial production.' Consequently, in less than 15 years, the Cumberland, the Dorset Gold Tip, the Yorkshire Blue and White and the Lincolnshire Curly Coat breeds were all lost forever. The remaining traditional breeds, such as the Berkshire, British Saddleback, Gloucestershire Old Spots, Large Black, Middle White and Tamworth, were little more than living relics displayed at agricultural shows.

Thankfully, by the late 1970s a few people saw sense and the Rare Breeds Survival Trust (RBST) was established in 1973. The work to preserve these breeds continues today with a 'use it or lose it' approach. Despite meat-lovers seeking them out, many of our traditional breeds are still listed as 'vulnerable' (200–300 animals left) or 'at risk' (300–500) by the RBST. So, the best thing you can do to stop these breeds going the way of the dodo is to eat them.

KEEPING PIGS

If you've got the space, the time and the effort, keeping pigs can be very rewarding. You'll also have meat that you've raised, butchered and cooked yourself. For more about how to do it see the *Pig Manual*.

Haynes
Pig
Manual
The complete
step-by-step guide
to keeping pigs

Liz Shankland

Consequently it's now the oldest pure English breed. Its hair makes it unpopular with many abattoirs and litter size can vary greatly, but the taste is fantastic – almost boar-like.

Berkshire

A small, black-skinned animal with white socks. This breed enjoyed royal patronage from Queen Victoria and was exported to America during the 1820s. When white pigs became popular after World War Two, numbers of the Berkshire breed declined. Today, it is still threatened with extinction. It is remarkably popular in Japan, where its meat is highly prized.

Saddlebacks

A large, lop-eared, black-bodied pig with a distinctive white 'saddle' across its shoulders. They're actually an amalgamation of two historical breeds: the Wessex Saddleback, originally from the New Forest, and the Essex, found in East Anglia.

Oxford Sandy And Blacks

A medium- to large-sized, multi-purpose animal, which is sometimes known as the 'plum pudding' pig due to its blondish red and black colouring. Produces succulent pork, high-quality bacon and good hams, and grows faster than many other traditional breeds.

A POTTED HISTORY OF THE ENGLISH PIG

Unlike horses, cattle and even dogs, historically, pig breeds were not thought worthy of much detailed classification. The pig was a working peasant's animal that was kept out the back of his croft or cottage and allowed to forage on 'mast' (fallen acorns and nuts from woodland), kitchen scraps, whey from cheese making and even dishwater! Pigs were thought of as 'loathsome but necessary' – just mundane parts of the everyday rural landscape. The killing of them in early winter, however, enabled the family to survive the cold. So while they may not have been of interest to learned men of animal science, they were very important to the working man. For much more detail, a really good read on the subject is *The English Pig: A History* by Robert Malcolmson and Stephanos Mastoris.

Main cuts of pork

HEAD

Use to make brawn and pâté; the cheeks are some of the best meat on the animal, as are the nuggets of meat in the temple and snout. Behind the head is the neck, which is good for mincing. The ears can be eaten too.

FOREQUARTER

Parts 2, 3 and 4 together form the forequarter, which can be cut into a number of pieces. The uppermost piece (2) is called the spare rib or shoulder and has a good amount of fat in it. This is the cut to use for pulled pork. It can be boned and rolled too.

Below that is the blade (3), which contains the shoulder blade. It's good for boning, rolling and stuffing.

Finally, towards the lower part is the hand or spring. This can be placed on a bed of stuffing and slow-roasted.

LOIN

Moving to the middle of the animal, we have the loin on top. There are many cuts, chops and steaks for this area.

The meat from the rib area with the ribs attached makes a great rack of pork, or the ribs can be removed and the meat rolled. This is a premium, but very tasty cut. Ask your butcher to chine it. Loin chops come from the middle of the loin, while chump chops come from the end, towards the rear leg. At the very end of the loin, just before the leg, is the chump.

Inside the animal is the fillet, which is called tenderloin on pigs. It's very tender, and like fillet, needs very gentle cooking.

BELLY

Below the loin is the belly. It has a 'thick end' towards the front legs and a 'thin end' towards the rear. The ribs extend down from the loin, and this is where 'rack of ribs' is found. Can be roasted whole and then cut into individual ribs.

LEG

The final third of the animal is the hindquarter. This large area is comparatively lean compared to other bits of the animal. The leg can be roasted or cut into steaks. The lower part can also be roasted if you want something smaller.

HOCK AND TROTTER

Finally there's the hock and trotter. The hocks can be smoked, and are great in soups. They can also be slow-roasted, as they have a good amount of fat in them. The trotters are best used in stocks, though in Italy they bone them out, stuff them and serve with lentils in a dish called zampone.

OTHER

Pork liver is used in pâtés and terrines, while the kidneys can feature in steak and kidney pies.

Bacon

Bacon, the most powerful meat known to man. Infamous for scuppering politicians' leadership ambitions and 'turning' vegetarians back to eating meat. It is, indeed, fantastic stuff.

EWW, WHAT'S THAT WHITE GOO?

Sadly, much bacon isn't what is used to be. Instead of a thick-cut, juicy rasher, most supermarket bacon is utter rubbish. When any meat cures, it loses weight. So some people soon realised that injecting the loins with salty water not only 'cured' the meat quicker, but also increased the weight again. That's what you're getting when you buy cheap bacon: salty water. This brine then oozes out in the pan during cooking in horrible white globs. Do not buy it, instead always look for dry cured bacon.

CURING BACON

Bacon is a cured meat, but what does curing actually mean? Well, it's the process of applying salt (and in the modern world a few other things) to meat to draw out the moisture and preserve it. Today, nitrates – specifically saltpetre – is added; it's a preserving agent that kills bacteria. It also helps keep the meat pink.

TYPES OF BACON

There are two main types of bacon sold in the UK: back bacon and streaky bacon, and they both come from the middle of the animal. Back bacon comes from the loin and includes the large eye of the meat and a little 'tail' of the start of the belly. Streaky bacon, meanwhile, is made solely from the belly piece of meat.

If you're making a bacon sandwich, make sure you cook the rind well on back bacon so it's crispy rather than floppy. There's nothing worse in a bacon butty than biting into it and finding you're unable to bite through the rind.

There is a third type, collar bacon, made from the neck end of the pig. It is unusual, in that it is rindless.

TYPES OF CURE

Dry cured is just that, the bacon is rubbed with salt and left to age. Wet curing sees the meat placed in a brining solution.

Proper wet curing (as opposed to just injecting the meat with brine) has certain advantages – this is known as the Wiltshire cure and was invented in that county by George Harris in the 1860s. It gave a milder, saltier flavour to the meat. Suffolk, too, has a long tradition of a type of wet curing to produce its famous black bacon. The sides are marinated in dark porter beer, molasses and brown sugar before being hot smoked for 2–3 days. The result is stunning.

Cold smoking is an extra stage done after curing, and for my money, smoked beats unsmoked every time. The cured sides are placed in a smoker with a small smouldering line of sawdust, often laid out in a line like a trail of gunpowder in a Western. It's not a fire as such, but is just enough to keep going for 6–10 hours and release enough smoke to flavour the meat.

Hot smoking sees a more intense fire that actually cooks the meat through, though of course, you can cook it again when you get home.

SOME OTHER CURED PIG PRODUCE

Lardo: this is back fat cured in rosemary and other herbs and spices from central Italy. It has an almost translucent quality, served thinly sliced as an antipasto.
Pancetta: this is made from belly pork and often diced into cubes.

HOW TO CURE YOUR OWN BACON

Go online and buy something called 'Prague Powder #1'. It's a blend of sodium nitrate and salt. You still need extra salt on top of this, but having the nitrate blended with the salt means it's safer and easier to portion out.

Follow the included instructions and apply with extra salt to your piece of meat. Seal in a ziplock bag or, even better, a vac packer and turn in the fridge every day. After a week, remove and quickly wash off any excess cure. Other flavouring kits are available that include herbs, sugar and such.

Always wear disposable gloves when handling cures and remember that cures penetrate muscle quicker than they do fat or skin, so apply less on the flesh side.

BRINGING HOME THE BACON

A side of bacon is called a 'flitch' and every year in Great Dunmow, Essex, there takes place the 'Dunmow Flitch Trials'. These date back to medieval times, and a reference to them appears in Chaucer's *The Wife of Bath* in *The Canterbury Tales*.

A prize of a 'flitch' of bacon goes to any married couple who can prove their devotion to the Judge and jury of six maidens and six bachelors from the Parish, convincing them that in 'twelvemonth and a day', they have 'not wisht themselves unmarried again'. See www.dunmowflitchtrials.co.uk if you and your spouse would like to take part!

Ham

Curing is also used in ham production. Whereas bacon comes from the middle section, ham come from the hind legs. Gammon is more akin to bacon, and unlike ham, must be cooked (either boiled or roasted) before eating.

England once produced hams that rivalled anything on the Continent. Sadly we don't seem to value our ham heritage as much these days. Nearly all Continental cured meats and hams have European PDO or PGI status, meaning they must be made in a certain way in a defined area.

YORK HAM

The King of British hams and now rare as hens' teeth. Made from the Large White and cured in salt and brown sugar for three months before ageing for anything up to two years, it can (or could) be smoked or unsmoked. A sad sight greeted me when I approached Scott's butchers in the ancient city of York. 'Closing down', the last maker of York hams within the shadow of the minster was gone. It's now a boutique children's clothes shop.

BRADENHAM HAM

Found in the counties of Wiltshire, Buckinghamshire and Shropshire, it is wet-cured in molasses, coriander and juniper berries.

JAMÓN SERRANO

This ham comes from Spain and sees the legs covered in salt for a fortnight, followed by 6 months' drying, before another 6–18 months' further drying. This process tends to happen at cooler, higher altitudes, hence the name 'serrano', meaning from the sierra or mountains.

JAMÓN IBÉRICO

Another ham from Spain, and indeed Portugal, made using only the meat from the Black Iberian pig. The production process is similar to serrano ham, but what differs is not only the breed, but also the diet. The best *jamón ibérico de bellota* comes from pigs that roam the oak forests eating acorns and is cured for 36 months.

JAMBON DE BAYONNE

Salted and air-dried, this ham has a sweetish taste and hails from the south-west of France.

PROSCIUTTO

Italian ham made from the leg. It is salted then pressed to drain away any remaining moisture. Washed, dried and aged for anything up to 18 months.

PRESUNTO

Similar to prosciutto, but from Portugal.

SPECK

From northern Italy on the German border, this ham is again a cured leg, but flavoured with aromatics including garlic, bay leaves, juniper berries, nutmeg and other spices. It is then lightly smoked.

BLACK FOREST HAM

Salted with aromatics similar to those for speck, a Black Forest ham is smoked for much longer, gaining an almost black exterior.

Sausages of Britain

It may surprise you to know that there are over 470 different flavours and varieties of sausage in the UK (Germany boasts around 1,000), and they're one of the few foods you can eat at breakfast, lunch and dinner. Here are just a few of the most popular ones:

BRITISH PORK SAUSAGE

A classic breakfast sausage featuring finely ground pork with a little rusk added to bind.

LINCOLNSHIRE SAUSAGE

A standard-sized sausage made with coarsely ground pork. Predominant flavouring is sage, as well as salt and pepper.

CUMBERLAND SAUSAGE

A large, thick sausage from Cumbria; highly spiced with white and black pepper, nutmeg and mace and served in a coil. Meat content should be around 80% and coarsely ground. Traditionally they were sold by length, so a good Cumberland sausage should be at least a foot long when uncoiled.

GLAMORGAN SAUSAGE

A Welsh 'sausage' made with Caerphilly cheese bound with egg or cold mashed potato and coated in breadcrumbs. Great for that one vegetarian person you occasionally find at your table.

LORNE SAUSAGE

A Scottish sausage made from beef and/or pork that's seldom seen south of the border. Made by adding the meat to a loaf-tin, setting firm and then cutting into slices, which are then fried or grilled.

JUMBO SAUSAGE

A larger, longer version of any traditional sausage. Bad examples are often found battered in fish and chip shops.

NEWMARKET SAUSAGE

An East Anglian sausage recipe, which now has Protected Geographical Indication (PGI) status. Made in slightly different ways by three firms in the town.

HISTORICAL SAUSAGES

Marylebone sausages from London were made with mace, ginger and sage, while Epping sausages were skinless and contained sage, lemon and nutmeg. Both Cambridge and Oxford have a sausage named after them. Oxford's were skinless, made with veal, beef suet and breadcrumbs and had sage and pepper as a flavouring. Cambridge's meanwhile opt for cooked, ground rice instead of breadcrumbs, with lemon sometimes joining the pepper and nutmeg.

BRITISH BEEF SAUSAGES

These are becoming more popular with people who do not eat pork. Most butchers now stock a beef variety.

FAGGOTS

These are made from minced pork, chopped pig's heart, liver, onion, seasoning and sometimes breadcrumbs. The resulting patties are then wrapped in caul fat (a thin membrane which surrounds the animals' internal organs). They're known in the north of England as savoury ducks, while a similar dish in France is called *crépinette*.

BLACK PUDDING

Food of the Gods; I love the stuff. Fat, cereal and pigs' blood, what's not to like? Extra flavourings include pepper and the herb, pennyroyal. Normally sliced and fried, the people of Bury instead boil them whole and then split and eat them with a blob of piccalilli.

HAGGIS

Sheep offal and barley encased in a sheep's stomach, much beloved north of the border, though, once every few years someone claims it was actually invented anywhere but there. Who cares? It's delicious and has its own poem to go with it.

Some popular international sausages

BOEREWORS

A popular sausage from South Africa made from coarsely ground beef, and occasionally lamb. Heavily spiced with nutmeg, clove, allspice and vinegar and coiled up like a Cumberland sausage. Key part of a *braai*, or South African barbecue.

FRANKFURTER

The most famous German sausage made from finely ground pork in a sheep casing to give a thinner sausage. Once made it is often smoked.

BRATWURST

A sausage made from pork and/or veal. There are over 40 varieties in Germany; some versions are whitish in appearance.

TOULOUSE SAUSAGE

A French sausage made from coarsely chopped pork and pepper. UK versions often contain garlic and wine (because they're French right?!) but many French versions omit these flavours.

CHORIZO

Spain's most famous sausage; highly spiced with smoked paprika. There are many different regional variations found all over the country.

MERGUEZ

A spicy sausage from North Africa made with lamb or beef in sheep casings and flavoured with paprika. Has a high meat content and no binder.

SAUSAGE FACTS:

- Sausages are known as 'bangers' because, from as far back as the 1910s, poorly made sausages would be composed of so much water, which would turn to steam during cooking and burst through the casing with a bang. This went national during World War Two, when meat was severely rationed and sausages really were terrible.
- Botulism is a potentially fatal disease that is thankfully rare, but it can be caught via poorly kept or produced food. It was first discovered in the 18th century and its name is derived from the German *Botulismus*, from the Latin for sausage. It was once known as 'sausage poisoning' due to poorly made German sausages. Interestingly, the last and biggest outbreak in the UK occurred in tubs of hazelnut yoghurt.

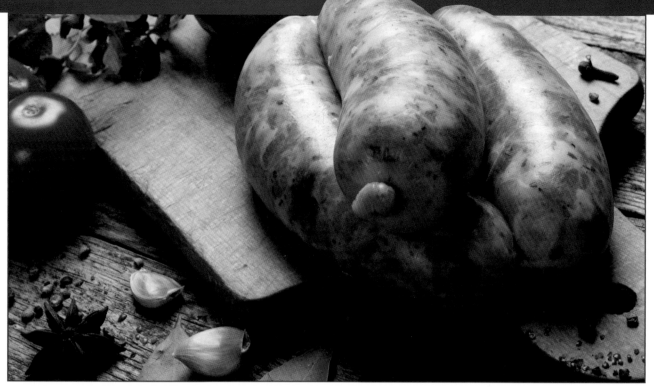

Sausage recipe

This basic recipe produces a good 'all rounder' sausage that's great for breakfast, lunch and dinner. It's a good one to practise if you're new to sausage making, and then build on as you become more experienced.

INGREDIENTS

- Approx. 1kg minced pork (a combination of fattier and leaner cuts)
- 1 tablespoon of fresh sage, finely chopped
- 100g breadcrumbs or rusk
- 150ml ice cold water
- 10g salt
- 5g black pepper
- 5g nutmeg
- Approx. 1.5m of hog casing

SAUSAGE-MAKING TIPS:

- **A rough rule of thumb is that around a kilo of meat fills around a metre of casing to give a good, thick sausage.**
- **To get the last of the meat out of the grinder, place chunks of sliced white bread in: this will force out the last of the meat. Grind this into a separate bowl, though.**

MEAT

For sausages, you want a mixture of lean and fatty meat. I tend to work on a ratio of around half as much fat to lean. For pork sausages, I use a combination of belly and shoulder. However, ask your butcher for any trim, off-cuts, or anything else that *he'd* normally put into his sausages – he might give you this cheaper. You can then mince all this up at home.

CASING

I'd recommend using only natural casings, as in the intestines of a pig. Artificial casings are made from collagen (usually derived from beef) and can be kept at room temperature. Natural casings are fresh and have to be kept chilled. You can tell a sausage with an artificial casing, as they're often straight, whereas a sausage made with a natural casing will bend into a gentle curve when cooking.

VARIABLES

You can really play about here. Swap out water for beer, or add your favourite herbs and spices. Other ingredients, such as garlic, honey, onion marmalade and even hard cheese, such as Parmesan, can be added (I wouldn't recommend all those in the one sausage though, might be overkill!). Fennel, chilli, garlic and a little pepper make a nice combination – not a breakfast sausage, mind!

How to make your own sausages

Most meat grinders and attachments come with fixtures and fittings that enable you to make your own sausages. This is really good fun and lets you and your family get all *Generation Game*. I've got an electric one from Lakeland that's great. Making sausages takes a little practice, but take it slow and keep everything clean and cold, and you won't go far wrong.

SPICY SAUSAGES

I'm using sage, paprika and chilli in this step-by-step, but really you can use anything.

1 Keep everything as cold as possible. Dice the meat into cubes, place them in a large bowl, and put that and the grinder attachments in the freezer for 30 minutes to chill right down. The colder the meat is, the firmer it'll be, meaning it will 'cut' better when it hits the plate. If it's warm and flaccid it'll just smear and stretch rather than cut. Keeping everything cold helps with hygiene too.

2 Most grinders come with two plates: coarse and fine (some have three). For sausages, I like to grind on the coarse plate. Prepare your grinder and bowl (the one that's been in the freezer so it, too, is cold). Refresh the hog casings in water for 10 minutes.

3 Start the machine. Feed in the meat pieces and allow the ground meat to fall into the bowl. Needless to say, be careful of long hair, loose clothing and your fingers. When all the meat is ground, mix in your herbs and spices and combine and then add the breadcrumbs and any water if you think it needs it (or experiment with other liquids) and recombine. The mixture should now be firmer. For smoother-textured sausages put the ground meat mixture through the grinder again with the coarse plate, then place in the fridge.

4 Remove the plate and fit the tubular sausage attachment to the grinder (my model includes a separator ring). Slide the hog skin on to the attachment so it's all bunched up at the far end. This is, perhaps, a task best performed out of sight of those with a delicate disposition.

5 Place a tray or plate under the grinder to catch your sausages. Feed the ground meat mixture slowly into the grinder with one hand, while holding the resulting sausage with the other, allowing it to fall down onto the plate. Don't worry too much about air pockets, you can snip them out later.

6 You can just coil up your sausage, Cumberland or boerewors style, or twist every 10cm and snip into individual sausages. Butchers only make them in long chains so they're easier to hang and move about. If you want to do that, pinch and twist as before, but loop every third sausage through the other previous two.

Roast loin of pork, and the best crackling in the world

Right – recipe time. This is my pork showstopper; it's a lovely cut that can feed plenty of people with a nice, thick, juicy slice of pork, as well as perfect crackling to go with it.

INGREDIENTS

Allow 1 rib per person

- Pork loin
- 2 lemons
- Free-pouring table salt (no need for sea salt for this)

For the veg bed (optional)

- 2 large carrots, roughly chopped
- 2 onions, skin on, quartered
- 1 stick of celery, chopped
- Half a glass of water, a light beer or white wine

THE MEAT

Ask your butcher for a chined loin of pork, un-scored (as in 'don't slash the skin') – that's very important. Most butchers score skin a few times about 1cm apart and far too deeply, I think. That's okay, but you'll get a better result by scoring it yourself using the method below. Plus it's one less job for him to do, which he'll like.

FRENCH TRIM

You can either ask your butcher to French trim the loin, or do it yourself. If you ask the butcher, make sure he gives you the trimmings, which can be used for stock or added to homemade baked beans (page 161). If you're going to French trim it, cut first 4cm down from the edge along the skin side, into the flesh and down to the bones. You then want to turn the loin over and cut each 'chunk' of flesh out from between each rib. After each piece comes out, scrape the bones clean.

CHINING

Chining is the act of pre-cutting along the ribs of the loin where they meet the spine. Doing this makes it much easier for you to carve the meat when it's roasted. If you've got a hacksaw (with a new, clean blade or special meat blade), you can have a go yourself. Don't cut too far into the eye of the meat, just across the base of the ribs.

PERFECT CRACKLING

Let's face it; it's one of the best bits on the pig. Follow this technique to the letter and you'll have the sort of crackling that makes a crunch so loud in your head you can't hear what other people at the table are saying.

I'd like to say I learned this technique in a far-off mystical land or at the foot of a world-renowned chef, but in fact, it was taught to me by a Chinese chef in Harrogate, Yorkshire. It's a three-day process; you can bring it down to 48 hours if you're in a rush, but roast loin of pork isn't a 'just popped round' midweek supper, it's something that's in the diary. So if you want this for Sunday lunch, start it on Friday morning before work.

METHOD

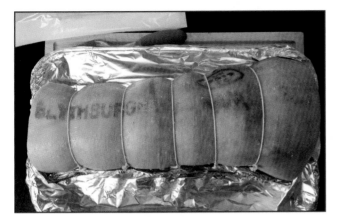

1 Find a roasting dish large enough to hold the pork; this will be its home for the next two days. Remove, place the pork on a chopping board and start to score the skin. I use a craft knife with an extendable blade. The advantage of this is you can just poke out the first 3–5mm of the blade. If you've not got one of these, use a scalpel or Stanley knife with a clean blade. Remember, you want to score the top layer of the skin a mere 3–5mm deep, not all the way through – you're almost scratching it. Repeatedly score the skin over and over again a few mm apart in the same direction, top to bottom.

2 Squeeze the lemons into a cup or small dish and using a pastry brush, coat the skin with the lemon juice. Then gently dust over the salt, which should start to dissolve when it hits the lemon juice. Place in the fridge uncovered.

3 The next day, do the same thing twice more: morning and evening, brush with lemon juice and dust with salt. Repeat once again on the morning of the day you want to roast it.

Roasting

4 If you want to make gravy then line the bottom of the roasting tray with the chopped vegetables and add the liquid.

5 Next take a long piece of tin foil and cover the French-trimmed rib bones (this stops them from colouring too much during cooking).

6 Place the pork in the tray, on top of the vegetables, with the ribs facing down into the tray. Using two more long pieces of tin foil, fashion a protective tent around the pork, leaving only the scored skin exposed. This stops the underlying meat from drying out, keeping it juicy while cooking.

7 Heat the oven to full whack, 220°C+. Place the pork on the middle shelf of the oven and leave for 10 minutes. Then turn down to 180°C and cook for around 80 minutes, depending on how big your loin is. Check the pork with your meat thermometer after an hour. Leave it to rest somewhere warm for 15 minutes before carving. Don't cover it, though, or you'll make the skin soggy.

To serve

8 The skin will have ballooned up from the surface of the meat, with a nice layer of fat in-between. Using a sharp knife, remove the crackling from the meat in one piece and carve the meat into chops.

9 Cut the crackling into pieces and serve.

'The crocodile'

An 'off menu' invention from Humphreys, my local butcher. The 'Saffron Walden crocodile' doesn't contain any crocodile, but instead calls for a 3cm thick pork loin chop slit open to make a pocket and a pork sausage stuffed inside. No one's quite sure why it got its name – the best answer is that it's as if the chop has eaten the sausage. Though the name does give us the opportunity to dust off that old joke, 'one crocodile please, and make it snappy'.

This is just another variation on the traditional 'carpetbagger steak' from 19th-century America. A 'carpetbagger' was a sort of travelling salesman/conman who carried around a large bag from which he sold things. Carpetbagger steak calls for a large, thick steak to be slit open to make a pocket and a seasoned, raw oyster placed inside. It's then grilled as normal. Chicken cordon bleu is another example of this technique.

METHOD

1 Slit the eye of the chop open with a small knife and make a pocket.

INGREDIENTS

- 1 large, 3cm thick pork loin chop, bone removed
- 1 good-quality pork sausage
- Butcher's string or elasticated ties (you can get these from your butcher)

2 Gently insert the sausage. If it's too big, twist the end to reduce the length and snip off with scissors.

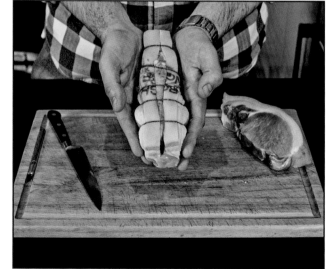

3 Secure in place with butcher's elastic bands or twine. The chop should be big enough to stand up with the eye of the meat facing down and the rind facing up.

Head cheese / brawn

If you can get your hands on a head and a couple of trotters, this is the dish to make. It's called 'cheese' because in the past it would have been pressed, just like curds were in times past to make what we now think of as cheese. It's important to get the herbs and seasoning right in this recipe so there's a fresher flavour to contrast the richness of the meat.

INGREDIENTS
- 1 pig's head, cleaned (rinse in plenty of cold water) and split into two
- 2 trotters, cleaned
- 2 onions, quartered
- 1 stick of celery
- 1 carrot, chopped
- 2 cloves of garlic, crushed
- 1 bunch of sage, chopped
- 1 bunch of parsley, chopped
- 1 teaspoon of black peppercorns
- 1 teaspoon of salt

METHOD
1 Rinse the head (pay particular attention to the pig's ears!) and the trotters and place in your biggest pan with all the other ingredients, apart from the herbs.
2 Bring to a boil then reduce to a simmer. Skim off any scum or foam that rises to the top.
3 Cook on a low heat for 4 hours until the meat falls off the bones. Leave to cool in the stock.
4 Lift out any bones or root vegetables and place your biggest bowl or clean bucket in the sink. Strain the meat and stock into a sieve and set aside the solid bits.
5 Now return the cooking liquid to the pan. Note how full it is and put it on a high heat to reduce by half, again, removing any scum or bits that float to the top.
6 Pick over the cooled meat and remove and discard all bones, skin and remaining vegetables. Pay particular attention to the snout, temple and cheeks – there is much meat to be found here. Roughly chop the remaining meat, season with salt and lots of freshly ground black pepper and combine with the chopped herbs.
7 Think about what you're going to make this in: a loaf tin (metal or ceramic) would be good, but you can use pudding bowls or ramekins, too.
8 Once your cooking liquor has reduced by half, return the seasoned meat to the stock and stir well. Place in your chosen container and leave to set in a cool place like a garage or cellar until the jelly has set. Covered in cling film, it'll keep in the fridge for a good few days.
9 When you want to serve, warm the container in warm water to loosen the brawn and turn out onto a plate, or just have it with a spoon. Best served with mustard, gherkins, butter, and hot sourdough toast.

A proper fry-up

Seb Emina, author of *The Breakfast Bible*, believes there should be nine things in a fry-up. They are as follows: eggs (fried), bacon, sausage, mushrooms, tomatoes, black pudding, toast, baked beans and some form of potatoes. Now, I can take or leave tomatoes and am not fussed about sugary baked beans either. I regard hash browns as a complete abomination, though bubble and squeak is allowed, or indeed slices of fried jacket potato. Fried bread, however, is a yearly indulgence – and only if there's proper bacon fat to fry it in. I have also, on one occasion, added kidneys. Gammon or lamb chops takes us into mixed grill territory. Finally the sauce must be brown, please folks.

If you're in Wales, however, you might add laverbread or cockles, while in Scotland there's fried haggis on the plate. Northern Ireland has the 'Ulster Fry', which adds a farl, potato cake and maybe a Scotch pancake, as well as toast and potentially fried bread too – carb overload!

I've gone for a standard version here. However you like your fry-up, cooking one is all about timing: you have to bring lots of elements from three different cooking areas together at the same time. This, then, isn't so much a recipe as a suggested sequence of events and procedures.

INGREDIENTS

Serves 4

- 8 sausages
- 8 rashers of streaky bacon
- 4 portobello mushrooms
- 2 large tomatoes
- 4 large eggs
- 4 pieces of black pudding
- 4 slices of toast

. . . .

METHOD

1 You can either try to cook everything in the one pan, as I've done here, or make use of the grill for cooking the meat. Few grills are at eye level these days, however – and I don't know about you, but I don't want to be doing half a dozen squats to cook my breakfast! Also, out of sight can sometimes lead to out of mind.

2 Cook in this order: meat, vegetables, eggs and then toast. So, let's start with the sausages. The key to cooking a sausage in a pan is to have it on a gentle heat – if it's too hot, your sausages are likely to burst or burn, or both. Go slow and steady. Tongs will help you to move the sausages over; you'll want to flip them over a couple of times. I also push them up against the lip of the pan; this helps to get some colour on the outside edge. Once the sausages are cooked, remove them and transfer them to a warm plate, lined with kitchen paper.

3 Crank up the heat and add the bacon to the pan, pressing down on the rind to release some of the fat.

4 While the bacon's cooking, slice the tomatoes in half and slice the mushrooms.

5 Once the bacon's cooked, remove to the warm plate along with the sausages.

6 Add the sliced mushrooms and tomatoes, cut side down, to the pan. You might need to add a little more oil. Cook through until the mushrooms are soft and turn the tomatoes once.

7 When the mushrooms are cooked, set aside, wipe out the pan, add some more oil and fry the eggs, or use a separate egg pan.

How to fry eggs

8 I like my eggs to have smooth white and a bright yellow, runny yolk. I'm not a fan of over-cooked eggs with a brown crunchy edge. I've tried various ways and think that generally it's best to buy a small egg pan and cook each egg individually. If you've not got one, do the following: crack the egg into a saucer and then slide it into the warm oil; you don't want the oil too hot. Slightly older eggs are better, as they'll run less. Place the lid on the frying pan; this helps direct the heat to the top of the egg.

9 Finally, get the toast on. You want this to be the last thing you bring to the table, as it's liable to go cold first.

WHAT'S FOR BREAKFAST?

The large cooked breakfast is a 19th-century invention of industrial Britain, and came into being as other meals during the day moved around. In the 16th century, the main meal of the day, dinner, was taken around 11am, but by the 18th century this moved to the evening, creating the need for not only breakfast, but lunch as well.

Your position in society governed when and what you had for breakfast. If you were a common labourer, you might have a sort of porridge eaten in the field (you would have been at work just after dawn).

If you were the gentry, however, you might swan downstairs at 10am and help yourself to a sideboard groaning with sausages, cold meats, bacon, kidneys, eggs and toast. We still see the legacy of this buffet approach in hotels. Indeed, breakfast in large country houses was a spectacle, where you might discuss matters of the day, answer letters and conduct business.

Pork tenderloin

Pork tenderloin is the equivalent of fillet steak on a cow, but much, much cheaper. Like fillet, there's very little fat, just soft juicy meat. It's a delicate piece of meat that doesn't need a huge amount of cooking. Being rather small, it's best suited to bite-sized portions and works particularly well when used as a starter.

This recipe sees it split open and stuffed with spinach, pine nuts and raisins, which is a great combination, popular in Spain. Once you've got your head around the preparation technique, you can easily use other fillings, such as sautéed mushrooms and thyme, or mozzarella, basil and sun-dried tomato. This recipe for stuffed pork loin and pea puree will serve two as a starter.

. . . .

INGREDIENTS

- 10g pine nuts, toasted and roughly chopped
- 40g spinach (cooked weight – start with two large handfuls)
- 3 thin slices of serrano ham
- 200g pork tenderloin
- Sea salt and black pepper, to season
- 10g plump, golden raisins
- 100ml chicken stock
- 200g frozen peas
- Vegetable oil, for cooking
- 10g butter

. . . .

METHOD

1 First, prepare the pine nuts and spinach. In a dry frying pan, toast the pine nuts over a low heat until they just start to colour; keep them moving about so they don't catch. Then set aside. Add a tablespoon of water to the pan then add the spinach and wilt it down. When it's wilted, remove it, place it on kitchen paper and give it a good squeeze. You want to remove all the moisture. It's also possible to do this in a microwave.

2 Take the ham out of the fridge to bring it to room temperature – this will make it easy to separate. Portion out the other ingredients.

3 Take your pork tenderloin and using a sharp knife, make a slit down the middle of the meat, but do not cut all the way through. Cut again either side of this incision to gently open the meat out flat.

4 Season with salt and pepper and then lay your wilted spinach down the centre of the meat leaving exposed flesh either side.

Top with the raisins and toasted pine nuts. Do not overpack it. Lay a sheet of cling film over another board and place the serrano ham on top of that.

5 Turn the tenderloin by 90° and, using both hands, roll up tightly, ensuring no filling spills out at either end. Place onto the ham at one end and, using the cling film as a guide, roll up tightly (don't roll the cling film inside though!). Twist the ends of the cling film to tighten further and tie with a knot – you should end up with a nice sausage shape. Put this back in the fridge to settle down for 30 minutes.

6 Bring a large pan of water to the boil then turn down to a simmer. Drop the rolled pork sausage in and poach gently for about 10 minutes. Remove form the pan and cool down under cold water (up to this stage can all be made earlier) and then remove the cling film.

7 Heat the chicken stock in a small saucepan until reduced and thicker. Pour half into a cup and reserve, and then add the frozen peas. Cook until tender, season and blitz to a puree with a stick blender or in a mini food processor.

8 Heat a glug of olive oil in a small frying pan and add the butter: it should foam a little. Add the tenderloin sausage and roll around the pan, basting with the butter. You just want to colour the ham.

9 Remove the tenderloin sausage from the pan, let it rest for a few moments, and then slice into 3cm discs. Serve with a blob of the pea puree and pour over a small amount of the reserved chicken stock as a sauce.

Pulled pork

The pulling of pork is something of an eternal tug of war between various American States and regions – each of which claim to do it 'properly'. This leaves your average Brit befuddled: as food trends go, we're fairly new to the low-and-slow style of cooking.

INGREDIENTS

Serves 6–10, depending on portion size and if you offer rolls

- 2kg shoulder of pork, bone in

For the rub

- 2 tablespoons of smoked chilli flakes
- 1 tablespoon of smoked paprika
- 200g brown sugar
- 1 tablespoon of salt
- 100ml apple juice

This is a recipe to cook over coals if you've got: a) lots of time, b) the right equipment and c) good weather. It's good for 4–6 hours in your barbecue. Remember the coals will need at least an hour to get white hot. You'll also have to top up the coals on the hour, every hour. So if you want this for a late Sunday afternoon barbecue, start work on it on Friday evening because it'll need at least 24 hours for the rub to do its work too.

If it's cold, wet and you've not got a barbecue, you can use a domestic oven, but it won't have any of the smoky flavour that makes pulled pork so darn tasty.

METHOD

1 Combine all the rub ingredients together.
2 Put the pork in a roasting tin and rub the marinade all over the meat until it's completely covered. Cover with cling film or a plastic bag and leave in the fridge overnight.
3 Take out of the fridge an hour before you want to cook it, so you're not putting fridge-cold meat near hot coals. Get the barbecue lit (see page 21 – Cooking meat over fire) and once the coals are glowing white, push to one side. Place a metal tin in the space where the coals were to catch any drips from the pork, place the pork on the grill and cover with the lid. Set your phone or watch to remind you to top up the coals on the hour.
4 After 4 hours the meat should have a black, charred exterior. Leave it to rest for 20 minutes then flake it apart with two forks. Serve on a white roll with homemade 'slaw and barbecue sauce.

Faggots

The word faggot means a bundle of something; commonly sticks or wood held together with something. In this case it's not wood, but pork and offal held together with caul fat (a thin membrane which surrounds the animal's internal organs).

INGREDIENTS

Serves 4–6

For the faggots
- 2 teaspoons of lard
- 1 onion, finely chopped
- 1 pig's heart, minced
- 1 pig's liver, minced
- 800g minced pork belly
- 8 rashers of streaky bacon, minced
- Pinch of nutmeg
- Pinch of mace
- 1 teaspoon of chopped sage leaves
- Salt and pepper, to season
- Around 300g breadcrumbs
- 1 egg
- Splash of milk
- 1 large piece of caul fat

For the gravy
- 2 teaspoons of lard
- 1 large onion, roughly sliced
- 1 teaspoon of plain flour
- 200ml stock
- 1 teaspoon of wholegrain mustard

Faggots are popular in the Midlands and north of England, where they sometimes go by the name of 'savoury ducks'. They were a great way of using up fresh offal after the family pig was killed in late autumn. Pig's liver, though milder than ox liver, still has that offal tang that gives faggots their unique flavour and texture. Omit the offal and caul fat and you're just making meatballs!

You should be able to get caul fat (and indeed everything else) from your butcher if you give him enough notice. Faggots are much easier to make if you've got a meat grinder with a coarse plate fitted. If not, ask your butcher (nicely) to mince everything for you, or buy ready ground pork mince and chop the offal finely by hand with a knife.

The breadcrumbs can be made from any stale bread you've got; again, just blitz in a food processor. You could, at a push, use a food processor to make the meat mix, but don't overblitz it – you want tiny chunks, not a smooth paste.

METHOD

1 First, add the lard to a frying pan and gently fry the onion until soft, but not coloured. Transfer to a sheet of kitchen roll and dab dry.
2 Prepare the offal and meat: finely chop, blitz or pass through the grinder and into a bowl.
3 Add the cooled onion to the meat mix, as well as the herbs, spices, salt and pepper.
4 Add the breadcrumbs and the egg and combine with your hands – you don't want it too sloppy. Add a splash of the milk, if you think it needs it. The breadcrumbs will absorb the fat that comes from the meat when they cook.
5 Using your hands scoop up the mixture, roll into balls about the size of a snooker ball and place on a large plate.
6 Fill a tray with water and place the caul fat in the water to loosen it.
7 Gently remove the caul fat and spread out on a large chopping board to check there are no holes in it.
8 Using a sharp knife, cut the fat into squares large enough to enclose your meatballs. Wrap the balls in the caul fat until it's all used and set aside. You can put these back in the fridge for a while now to firm up.
9 Faggots are better braised in a little liquid rather than roasted dry; this helps keep them juicy. You can also serve them with this gravy: first, heat the oven to 160°C. Add the lard to a metal roasting tin (large enough to hold your faggots) and melt on the hob. Throw in the onions and fry gently until soft. Now add the flour to the fat and combine quickly before adding the stock and whisking. Finally, add the mustard.
10 Place your faggots in the gravy and, using a spoon, dribble some of the gravy over the top of each of them. Cover with foil and place in the oven for 1 hour. Remove the foil for the last 20 minutes of cooking. Serve with mash and peas – marrowfat ones preferably.

Pork ribs

Sticky subject, ribs, literally. There's lots you can play about with, but one of the most critical things you can do to make outstanding ribs is remove the membrane from the back of them.

Removing the membrane

INGREDIENTS
Serves 4–6
- 1 rack of ribs (around 1kg)

For the dry rub
- 1 teaspoon of cumin seeds
- 1 teaspoon of coriander seeds
- 1 tablespoon of soft brown sugar
- 2 teaspoons of smoked paprika
- 1 teaspoon of mustard
- 1 teaspoon of salt
- 1 teaspoon of dried oregano
- 1 teaspoon of black pepper

For the barbecue sauce
- 200ml ketchup
- 40ml water
- 50ml cider vinegar
- 2 tablespoons of light brown sugar
- 1 tablespoon of Worcestershire sauce
- 1 teaspoon of garlic powder
- Salt and pepper, to season

This is a two-stage process. Firstly a dry rub goes on the meat; it's best to leave this for 24 hours if you can. Then the ribs are slow-cooked, so the meat is falling off the bone. Barbecue sauce is applied for the final stage to make the ribs go nice and sticky.

METHOD

1 To make the dry rub, toast the cumin and coriander seeds in a dry frying pan, and then combine with all the other dry rub ingredients. Blitz in a coffee grinder or grind to a powder in a pestle and mortar.

2 Lay the ribs in a baking tray, prick with a fork and rub the dry rub all over both sides. Leave to marinate in the fridge overnight.

3 To make the barbecue sauce, mix all the ingredients in a pan over a low heat until thickened and set aside.

4 Heat the oven to 130°C and place the ribs in an oven dish, tightly sealed with foil. Cook for 2–2.5 hours, and then remove the foil. Crank up the heat, or switch to the grill, and brush the cooked ribs with about half of the barbecue sauce.

5 Place the ribs under the grill until they're nicely charred. These really are better done on a barbecue – you need long, slow, indirect heat to smoke the meat over several hours. You then adjust it for direct high heat to crisp up the ribs.

6 Serve with the rest of the barbecue sauce as a dip.

Scotch eggs

Egg, sausage meat and breadcrumbs. What's not to love about the Scotch egg? It's breakfast in a spherical form. You can really play with the components of a Scotch egg: I've seen versions with cheese in the middle, fish instead of pork meat and smashed-up crisps on the outside instead of breadcrumbs.

INGREDIENTS

Serves 4

- 6 eggs (2 are needed to stick the crumbs to the sausage meat)
- 1 tablespoon of plain flour on a saucer
- 200g pork mince
- 100g black pudding
- 2 sausages – meat squeezed out from the casings (or around 100g sausage meat)
- Salt and pepper, to season
- 150g fresh breadcrumbs

I've kept things fairly traditional for this version, but have made one little change. I've added black pudding to the sausage meat mix. This not only gives a darker layer, but a wonderful spicy flavour too. I've also gone for a mixture of pork mince and the contents of two sausages to help bind everything together. If black pudding's not your thing (what's wrong with you, man!) then replace with more pork mince and sausage meat, and add some finely chopped herbs.

The knack with Scotch eggs is getting the sausage meat cooked, while still keeping the yolk runny. For this, I swear by my boiled egg indicator widget. Put this in the pan with the eggs and it will change colour to tell you when they're done (normally around 5 minutes). I use medium eggs in this recipe; large ones will take a little longer. Once cooked, plunge into cold water to stop the cooking process, and peel. Drying the eggs thoroughly and rolling them in a little flour will help your pork mixture stick to them. Finally, you really have to deep fry Scotch eggs – baking doesn't work.

METHOD

1 Boil four of the eggs for 5 minutes then cool and gently peel. Place on kitchen roll to dry.
2 Place each egg in the saucer of flour and roll around to coat.

5 Beat the two remaining eggs together in a bowl. Place the breadcrumbs in another bowl next to them.

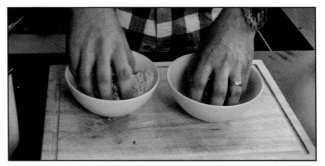

3 In a bowl, combine the pork mince, black pudding and sausage meat. Season, and mix well with your hands.
4 Scoop up a handful of the meat mixture and flatten into the palm of your hand. Carefully place the egg onto it and then wrap the egg in the meat mixture to cover it. You may need a little more of the meat mixture to cover it all. Repeat until all four eggs are wrapped in meat.

6 You'll want a 'wet' left hand and a 'dry' right hand. That way you coat the Scotch egg and not your fingers! Roll the meat ball in the beaten egg with your left hand, then transfer to the bowl with breadcrumbs in. With your right hand, cover and coat the egg completely with crumbs. Repeat for the other three eggs.
7 Heat the oven to 170°C; you'll put your eggs in here on kitchen paper to 'dry off' after frying.
8 Heat your oil in a chip pan or deep fat fryer to 160°C and fry each egg until the breadcrumbs are golden brown. Then place them in the oven for 10 minutes to finish cooking. You can eat them hot, or let them go cold. Fiery English mustard is by far the best condiment to serve with them.

Toad in the hole

Toad in the hole is one of those classic British dishes that helped a little meat go a long way. Indeed, Mrs Beeton describes it as 'a homely and savoury dish', the sort of thing for just the immediate family when money was tight. Of course, originally any leftover or cheaply bought bits of meat or offal were used.

The Victorian celebrity chef, Alexis Soyer, gives not one, but 11 recipes in his book, *A Shilling Cookery for the People*. Other potential 'toads' he suggests include; leftover fish, calves' brains, potatoes and even sparrows! Mercifully, sausages became the norm around the 1920s, and you'll be pleased to hear that's what I'm going with in my recipe. But it's clear you can put lots of things 'in a hole' – whole roasted courgettes or carrots, for example, or what about black pudding (would that be a black hole)? Rabbit meat would also have a certain irony.

You need a large metal tin rather than a ceramic one for this, as it'll transfer the heat better. You also need to get it very, very hot.

INGREDIENTS

Serves 6

- 2 eggs
- 150ml milk
- 100g plain flour
- Salt and pepper
- 70g lard
- 6 good-quality sausages with a high meat content

METHOD

1. Make the batter in a stand mixer or with a hand whisk. Crack the eggs into a bowl and beat, and then add the milk, flour and seasoning and whisk until fully combined. You're after something with the viscosity of cream. Place it in the fridge (you can do this stage up to 12 hours earlier).

2. Heat the oven to 220°C. Cook the sausages by gently frying them in a pan, turning them occasionally. Once cooked, set them aside on kitchen paper.

3. When your oven is hot, place the lard in the tin and put it in the oven to melt. You want it almost smoking (about 5–8 minutes).

4. Get the batter out of the fridge and have a ladle ready. Working quickly, take the tin from the oven and ladle out the batter. It should fizz and bubble. Place the sausages on top of the batter and put back in the oven.

5. Bake for about 25–30 minutes until puffed up and golden brown.

6. Best served with mash (page 154) and onion gravy (page 158), I think.

Roast sausages, onions and polenta

When you're feeding a lot and want something a bit different from mash (and a lot less faff to make), then reach for polenta. I like making it with milk and water rather than just water (though, you could use stock instead) and beating in butter, seasoning and lots of Parmesan.

This is basically a northern Italian version of sausage and mash. Italian fresh sausages are often flavoured with fennel seed; they're available from specialist Italian food shops or delis, or online, or make your own (see page 58). Top tip: look for a bag labelled cornmeal (often found in larger supermarkets' 'ethnic' section rather than polenta – it's exactly the same stuff, and often loads cheaper.

You'll need a roasting tin with a wire rack, as this will suspend the cooking sausages above the sauce (but allow any delicious fat to drip into it). If you've not got one, place the sausages in the stock with the onions, but turn during cooking so they roast both sides, rather than poach.

INGREDIENTS

Serves 6–8
- 1 fennel bulb
- Glug of vegetable oil
- 3 large onions, sliced
- 2 tomatoes, chopped
- 1 teaspoon of crushed fennel seeds (optional, but good if you're using British bangers)
- Salt and pepper, to season
- 250ml dark chicken or beef stock
- 8 large meaty sausages

For the polenta
- 400ml milk
- 1 litre water
- 300g yellow, coarse polenta or cornmeal
- 75g butter
- Pinch of salt
- 50g Parmesan cheese

METHOD

1 Take the fennel bulb and wrap it tightly in layers of cling film. Microwave on high power for 3–5 minutes (my thanks to Heston Blumenthal for this top tip) until soft. Leave until cool enough to handle. Then finely slice.

2 Heat the oven to 170ºC. Next, place the roasting tin on the hob and add the oil. Add the onions and fennel and cook on a very low heat until the onions have softened. Fennel takes longer to break down than onions, hence giving it a head start in the microwave first.

3 Add the diced tomatoes, fennel seeds (if using), seasoning and stock and bring to the boil.
   Carefully place the rack in the tray – it should stand above the sauce – then place your sausages on the rack.

4 Transfer to the oven to cook for 30 minutes, checking occasionally.

5 Next make the polenta. Put the milk and the water in a large saucepan or casserole. Bring to the boil then turn the heat down.

6 Add the polenta slowly, in small amounts, so it has a chance to incorporate in the water, while continually stirring with a whisk. When all the polenta has been added, continue to stir less frequently – around every 3 minutes – scraping it away from the edges of the pan to stop it catching. It should be done about the same time as the sausages take to cook – around 30 minutes.

7 Lastly, add the butter, seasoning and Parmesan and give it a final beating. Check a small amount – it should be creamy, but not too runny or gritty, and have a texture like scrambled eggs.

8 I think this is best served family style on a huge plate in the centre of the table. Add the polenta to a warm plate and spread out, place the sausages on top and then carefully remove the rack and pour over the sauce. Garnish with a little parsley if you like.

Honey-glazed Christmas ham

A Christmas classic – up there with *The Snowman*, bad jumpers and drunken in-laws. A good baked ham is something that should sit on every sideboard during the holidays.

Making a ham is a two-stage process (or three, if you're planning on starting right from scratch and brine a fresh piece of pork). First you boil it, then after removing the skin, score it and roast it with a glaze.

You need to decide how many this ham is going to feed. If you're also doing turkey, pork pie and all the trimmings over the festive period, you might want to buy a smaller joint. If not, go large.

SMOKED OR UNSMOKED?

I like smoked, but it depends how strong the smoke is and if you like the taste too. Ideally, you want something with a subtle waft of wood smoke, rather than overpowering it; sadly there's no way to really tell until you tuck in.

TO SOAK OR NOT TO SOAK?

In the past, many recipes recommended soaking the meat to remove any salt, but these days that's not really necessary, as hams aren't salted like they once were. Some cured versions are salted though, so it's worth checking when purchasing. If you do need or want to soak it, place it in a large, clean bucket or tub of cold water overnight.

A dish like this only works with a really good piece of meat, so it's down to the butcher for a quality piece of pig leg that's actually spent its life roaming about freely. Needless to say, this will be a big piece of flesh, so you'd better have a really big preserving pan or stockpot to hand. If you've not got one, ask for one for Christmas.

INGREDIENTS

- 3kg ham (bone in)
- 2 bay leaves
- 3 star anise
- Half the zest of an orange
- 2 onions, quartered
- 5 cloves
- A few peppercorns

For the glaze

- 2 tablespoons of mustard powder
- 4 tablespoons of brown sugar
- The other half of the zest of an orange
- 1 tablespoon of marmalade
- A squeeze of orange juice
- Handful of cloves

METHOD

1 Put your ham and the other ingredients, apart from the glaze ones, in a large stockpot and cover with cold water. Bring to the boil and skim off any scum that rises to the top, then turn down the heat to a gentle simmer and cook for 30 minutes per 450g (so an average 1.5kg joint would need 100 minutes). You may need to top up the water during cooking.

2 Meanwhile, make the glaze. Place the mustard and brown sugar in a bowl and combine. Add the orange zest and the marmalade, and then a little orange juice to loosen. You don't want it so stiff you can't paint it on the ham, or so runny it'll just slide off. Something with the consistency of thick custard is what you want.

3 Once the ham has cooked, remove it from the water (you can reduce this a bit more and use it as stock – it's great for cooking pulses) and leave to cool.

4 Once it's cool enough to handle, use a sharp knife to remove the rind, but not the layer of white fat underneath it.

5 Using a scalpel or craft knife score the fat in a criss-cross diamond design.

6 Using a pastry brush, paint the glaze onto the ham, ensuring you can still see the criss-cross cuts beneath. Once completely glazed, stud a clove into the centre of each diamond (this is traditional, but optional).

7 Heat the oven to 200°C and place the ham on a roasting tray. You're only really looking to caramelise the glaze, so around 20 minutes should do – keep an eye on it, mind, so that it doesn't catch and burn.

8 Leave to cool a little, then slice away when needed. It should last until twelfth night.

Pork katsu curry don

Curry – Victorian Britain's gift to the Japanese! In Japan, these dishes are known as *yōshoku* and became popular during the Meiji period (1868–1912) when Japan opened itself up to Western ideas, trade and food. Curry – specifically British-style curry – is so popular that it's served to the Japanese Navy on Fridays.

INGREDIENTS

Serves 4

- 4 pork cutlets or medallions, bone and fat removed, about 1cm thick
- 2 tablespoons of plain flour
- 2 beaten eggs
- 1 packet of panko breadcrumbs
- 1 small carrot
- 1 small green pepper
- 1 packet of Japanese curry sauce mix
- 2 litres sunflower or vegetable oil
- Sushi rice to serve, around 50g per person

This recipe is basically a Japanese version of a schnitzel served with curry sauce and rice. Tonkatsu means 'pork cutlet'; indeed, pork is Japan's most popular meat. But you can also make it with chicken.

This is one of my all-time favourite takeaways. There was a Japanese takeaway near where I used to live and I ordered this so much I could tell which of the two chefs was working that night by the way the vegetables were cut, as each had a slightly different way of doing it.

It's actually quite easy to make at home, and is great Friday night fodder. Consequently I don't recommend making the sauce from scratch; it won't have that oddly sweet and bland taste. That's an odd thing to say about 'curry' sauce, but here it's more like a spicy gravy. Look in the supermarket for a block of S&B Golden Curry sauce mix. These are sort of stock cube-like things that you just rehydrate with boiling water. It's best to deep fry the katsu, so bust out a wok filled with oil or your deep fat fryer.

METHOD

1. Cut the bone and the fat from a pork chop and flatten with a rolling pin, or have your butcher prepare it.
2. Dust each piece of pork in flour then shake to remove any excess. Using your left (wet) hand, place the pork in the beaten egg to coat it, and then transfer to the breadcrumbs. Coat the pork in crumbs and press them on firmly using just your right (dry) hand. Repeat for the other three pieces and set aside.
3. Peel and chop the carrot into small pieces, and do the same with the green pepper. Place the carrot pieces in a small saucepan, a third full of water, and bring to the boil then turn down to cook for about 5 minutes. Add the green pepper pieces. This water will be used to make your curry sauce, as per the packet's instructions.
4. Cook the rice according to the packet's instructions. Heat the oven to 100ºC.
5. Heat the oil in a wok or deep fat fryer to 170ºC and fry each pork katsu. Transfer to a plate lined with kitchen roll in the oven to keep warm.

Braised pigs' cheeks

Think about how much work a pig's cheeks do? All that chomping all day – that's why these hard-working muscles are one of the best bits on the animal, with fat that marbles the meat throughout.

However, they do need long, slow cooking in a liquid to get the best out of them; naturally I've gone for cider in this recipe. The result is a meat that is tender and gelatinous, so much so you can eat them with a spoon.

Pig cheeks are much easier to get hold of these days than they used to be. Ask your butcher for them, but even some supermarkets are now beginning to stock them. Depending on their size, I think – a bit like using tea bags – it's best to allow one per person and 'one for the pot', just in case you've got an appetite. Consequently, I've gone for a recipe that serves four here, so that's five cheeks.

INGREDIENTS
- 1 tablespoon of plain flour
- Salt and pepper, to season
- 1 tablespoon of lard
- 5 pigs' cheeks
- 2 large onions, peeled and sliced
- 2 dessert apples, peeled, cored and sliced
- 300ml cider
- 150ml stock
- 2 tablespoons of crème fraîche
- 1 teaspoon of wholegrain or Dijon mustard
- Chopped parsley, to serve

METHOD
1 Heat the oven to 160°C.
2 Put the flour on a plate and season with salt and pepper.
3 In a large casserole, melt the lard over a medium heat. Dust each cheek in the flour and then fry in the lard to get a little colour on its surface, before transferring to a clean plate. Repeat for the other cheeks.
4 Turn down the heat, add the sliced onion to the pan and cook until soft.
5 Return the cheeks to the pan, add the apple, cider, stock, crème fraîche and mustard, and combine.
6 Bring back to a gentle boil and place in the oven (you can cover with a cartouche if you like, see page 23).
7 Cook for around three hours, turning the cheeks occasionally to ensure a nice, even cooking. Garnish with the parsley and serve with mash, or even better, champ (see page 155).

CHAPTER 4
BEEF

In 1748, Pehr Kalm, a Swedish visitor to England, noted that 'the art of cooking as practised by Englishmen does not extend much beyond roast beef and plum pudding'. Well there's nothing wrong with doing a couple of things really well, eh Pehr?

Historically, the reason we're known for our splendid roast beef is that we had two things in abundance: great cattle and a lot of forest to provide wood. And those of you who've had 'proper' roast beef, cooked in front of a blazing fire, will know what I'm talking about. We may not have huge fires to roast our beef in front of these days, but we still produce excellent beef.

Types of cattle in the UK

With typical British grace, Victorian breeders sent their cattle creations all over the world. Beasts that now walk the grass plains of North and South America can trace at least some of their DNA back home to Blighty, the Stockyard of the world.

Indeed, when one of France's most famous butchers, Yves-Marie Le Bourdonnec, said in 2014, 'we have lost the notion in France of what a good steak is. The best rearers in the world are the British', he was expelled by the French butchers' federation.

So, all meat is basically British meat and the same – right? Wrong. There has been significant crossing, upgrading and general genetic jiggery-pokery with breeds from many countries over the centuries. What follows is what we consider our traditional British breeds. Yes, some like the Hereford were a result of adding a dash of Dutch blood.

Larger, faster-growing Continental beef breeds, such as Charolais, Limousin or Belgian Blue, began to arrive in the UK in the 1950s and 1960s, initially to improve the UK's dairy herd. Beef from these animals produces a carcass with less fat and a higher percentage of saleable product, which, until recently, is what the consumer demanded. Nowadays, things aren't as clear-cut.

ABERDEEN ANGUS

The poster boy of the beef world, and probably the breed that most people have heard of, if only due to the London-based tourist trap restaurant chain of the same name. Naturally polled (hornless) and known in the north-east of Scotland since the 16th century, they were improved in the 1820s, and soon found their way all over the world. Be careful, though, in the UK much Certified Aberdeen Angus meat comes in fact from crossbreeds (legally they have to be sired from a registered, pedigree bull). The rest of its genetic make-up can be from dairy animals or Continental breeds. Pure-bred Angus beef is available, but in small quantities. In the US it's even worse: Angus is just a trade name.

HIGHLAND

HIGHLAND

Lovely looking animals with big, shaggy coats (very much the Chewbacca of the bovine world) and two huge horns. Hard as nails and able to survive in harsh Scottish winters, they can eat pretty much anything too. Indeed, as one Scottish farmer once said to me, 'if you want some land clearing, put a "coo" on it'. Needless to say, the meat is stunning.

RED POLL

Bred in the 19th century in East Anglia by crossing the Norfolk Red beef cow with the Suffolk Dun dairy cow (both now extinct), this is a dual-purpose animal. They're also found in the West Country, as well as being one of the first breeds exported to the USA and Australia.

ABERDEEN ANGUS

RED POLL

LONGHORN

HEREFORD

LONGHORN

These multipurpose cattle are native to the north of England and would have been used to pull ploughs, as well as for milk and meat. They have brown-white dappled coats, while their distinctive curved horns were made into drinking vessels. The breed was improved and dedicated as a beef breed by the agriculturalist Robert Bakewell. He crossed these long-horned heifers with a Westmoreland bull resulting in a much larger animal known as the Dishley Longhorn. Not to be confused with a Texas Longhorn, which is originally from Spain.

GALLOWAY

Today, recognised as the oldest breed of beef cattle in the British Isles and native to south-west Scotland. They have a dark, thick coat, which like the Highland, helps protect them in the winter. The beef is juicy, tender and flavourful. They were once 'droved' in their hundreds from Scotland to England, as far south as East Anglia.

HEREFORD

Originally a draft animal (for pulling ploughs) it has in the past 300 years been bred for beef. These chunky, red cattle with white patches and a white face originate from, and are still found in, the Western counties of England (including Hereford). They're also found all over the globe.

DEXTER

These small cows are about half the size of a Hereford and originated from south-west Ireland, where they were known as the 'poor man's cow'. They were once extremely rare, both here in the UK and back in Ireland, but have had something of a resurgence recently, particularly with people interested in growing their own meat due to their easy temperament and small size. Indeed, Dexter meat has a good fat ratio and flavour. The best place to find Dexter beef is farm shops and butchers.

GALLOWAY

DEXTER

The five rules of beef

There are five main factors that contribute to the quality of the beef on your plate. Granted, some of these influence the final result less than others, but each has a part to play in ensuring you get something worth eating.

1. BREED

What breed of animal has the beef come from? I favour traditional breeds over Continental ones. A Dexter, for example, produces smaller cuts, yes, but they're packed with flavour.

2. FEED

Ask a child what cows eat and they'll say grass. The animal has four 'stomachs' designed exactly for this purpose. Cows are not designed to be intensively fed grain, soya and other foods that either a) we can eat, or b) cause wild habitats to be destroyed in order to grow them.

3. AGE

How has the carcass been aged? This is critically important to good beef, much more so than any of the other meats we eat. Age is flavour and texture – without it, it's just protein. Ageing meat is discussed in detail on page 83.

4. CUT

Are you using the right cut? You don't stew fillet steak; you don't flash-fry oxtail. Using the right bit of the animal for the right purpose is important. Not only that, but is it the right size?

5. COOK

Finally – and this is the bit you do have total control over at home – are you cooking it in the best possible way? Cooking times can vary depending on many things. Make sure your oven and other equipment is in good condition. A very basic rule for cooking most cuts of beef is either 'hot and quick' or 'low and slow'.

Age and beef

Age is flavour; naturally that applies in the hanging process, but just before we discuss that let's think about the age of the animal. Nearly all beef in Britain, apart from in a few very special producers, is slaughtered at 30 months old. This was introduced after the BSE crisis in the early 1990s (BSE does not develop fully in cattle until they are around this age). It was relaxed in 2006, but few cattle farmers raise meat OTM (over thirty months) as it costs them both in production, processing fees and red tape.

However, at the time of writing, elderly bovines are all the rage in London's meat-obsessed dining scene, and a number of restaurants are now selling meat from Basque and Spanish ex-dairy cows which can be up to 17 years old. The French filmmaker, Franck Ribière, searched the world for the best steak in his 2014 film *Steak (R)evolution*. He too, favoured the older cow. It remains to be seen if OTM meat has a more commercial future or remains a niche, high-end restaurant experience. But you can bet that if chefs start demanding it and we start buying it, farmers will start producing it.

Freshly killed beef isn't very edible, it can be tough and needs time to develop that rich, beef flavour. And the main and most effective way that happens is by ageing. There are two ways of doing this: the easy, rubbish way (wet ageing) and the hard, better way (dry ageing).

DRY AGEING

Dry ageing sees the carcass cut in half and hung in a chilled room (typically around 2°C) in which fans move air around and over the meat. The humidity and airflow must be carefully controlled; too warm and bacteria can grow, too cold and water in the meat will start to freeze rather than evaporate.

This process can be any time from two to seven weeks, though most stop around 28 days (four weeks). I once had an over 50-day-old piece of beef from a butcher that a customer had forgotten to collect. Once we'd cut the bloom off (a harmless bacterial growth on the outside of the meat), what was inside was incredible. Of course, some chefs and butchers keep going; 60- and 180-day varieties are available. In 2015, The Dallas Chop House, Texas, served a steak that was aged for 459 days, that's 15 months!

As well as the loss of moisture from the carcass, another thing that happens is that the natural enzymes present begin to break down the tissues in the meat; this makes the meat tenderer.

Dry ageing requires careful stock management and an experienced eye. Not only does it reduce the weight of the beef as the water evaporates (meaning there's less to sell), but butchers might also have to trim the externally exposed muscle due to discolouration. In all, up to 30% of the carcass weight can be lost during dry ageing.

WET AGEING

So, dry ageing gives better-tasting meat (studies have proved this, as has my mouth), but it requires skill and costs money – you can see why some bean counter somewhere wanted to do away with it. Enter wet ageing. This sees the beef vacuum-sealed in plastic bags and left to 'age' for between 7 and 14 days. Around 90% of the beef we eat in Britain is processed in this way. The result is a safe, transportable, easily storable, boring product that doesn't lose any weight. Another 'shortcut' used is running an electric current (known as electrical stimulation) through the meat to speed up the rigor mortis process.

It may be 'aged', in that it moved forward through time and can legally be described as, say, 28-day-old beef. But it's not matured; having sat in a bag of its own blood, it can never have the flavour profile of proper dry-aged beef.

So, ask your butcher if his meat is dry aged; ask to pop your head in his chiller room. Good butchers have nothing to hide and are proud of the care and attention they lavish on their meat. Age, specifically dry ageing, is a critical part of beef's unique flavour.

CAN I AGE MEAT AT HOME?

No, not unless you've got a chiller unit and dehumidifier. Of course some guys in the States have jury-rigged together a fridge and desk fan and had a go, but it's not really worth it. This is a job for your butcher.

Cuts of beef

You might be surprised to hear that there are actually many different ways to take apart a cow. Indeed different countries, even different regions within those countries, all cut up animals differently.

In 1954, the food writer Dorothy Hartley (her *Food In England* is my desert island tome) was still able to identify the 'Scotch cut', the 'Welsh method', the 'Yorkshire cut' and the 'South and London-counties cut'. This probably made sense when each region had its own specific breeds of cattle that needed slightly different treatment.

Today, most butchers, abattoirs and meat-processing plants adopt a standard way of butchering beef. Naturally, this being the UK, the process is thoroughly documented and each cut now has a number. 'Sirloin steaks, standard trim', for example, is Sirloin B006. You can search online for this document and have a read. It's brilliant, like Lego instructions for cows!

THE FOREQUARTER CUTS
Cheeks
Cows spend a lot of their time chewing, so their cheeks have a great flavour and texture. Best braised.

Neck
Also known as the clod, this is a tightly muscled area. The meat is mainly diced for stewing steak.

Chuck or blade
From the upper part of the shoulder, this can be boned and rolled. Good for marinating and slow-cooking for an economical roast.

Fore rib
Behind the chuck sits the fore rib, which are the first four or five ribs. This can be roasted whole, though it's fattier than the sirloin from the other eye. This is also where ribeye steaks come from.

Thin rib
These also go by the name short ribs, Jacob's ladder or oven busters. They're best braised. Found towards the back of the forequarter where it meets the middle and the ribs start.

Thick rib
Again, this cut has a number of names, such as shoulder, top rib and the oddly named leg of mutton cut (as it's said to resemble a leg of mutton in shape). Best pot- or slow-roasted. Can also be made into stewing steak.

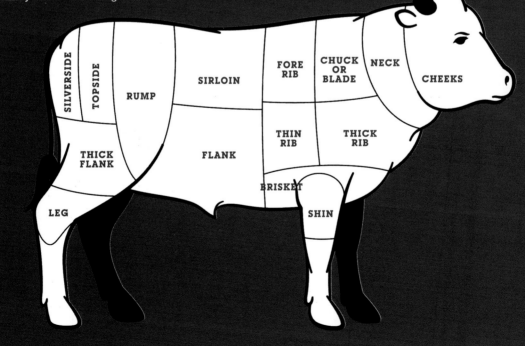

Brisket
Really flavourful when boned, rolled and slow-cooked, but is more commonly used to make salt beef or pickled beef.

Shin or foreshin
The front leg, it has a lovely tight, feathery texture and connective tissue. Makes amazing stews with a rich, gelatinous gravy.

THE MIDDLE
Sirloin
The most expensive part of the beast, which gives numerous steaks and whole joints, both on and off the bone. This is where steaks such as porterhouse, filet mignon and, of course, sirloin come from. Joints-wise it's home to wing rib and a whole boned and rolled sirloin.

Flank
Technically, this comes in two parts: the forequarter flank, which has ribs present, and the thin flank, which doesn't. Here you'll find the hanger steak and the bavette.

THE HINDQUARTERS
Rump
.The upper part of the rear of the animal. It's here we find rump steaks, which, if aged correctly, are some of the best on the animal thanks to all that walking about.

Silverside
Found towards the back of the rump, this gets it name from the silvery membrane found between the muscles. It's often sold as a cheap roasting joint (with a piece of fat tied on) but it's much better pot-roasted.

Topside
A good roasting joint, this can be slow-roasted and served pink, or pot-roasted. Other uses include flash-frying.

Thick flank
From the upper part of the leg, this can be pot-roasted as a joint or cut into strips and flash-fried. Can also be made into salt beef.

Oxtail
Very flavourful, if not very 'meaty' – sadly not as cheap as it once was. Great for adding oomph to stews, or for slow-cooking.

Leg
The back leg or shin, lean muscle. Known as the 'hough' in Scotland.

How to carve beef

How to carve beef depends on the cut you've roasted. What's critical, however – no matter what the cut is – is ensuring it's rested for a sufficient amount of time.

Get your knife as sharp as possible and try to carve the meat across the grain – this will make the meat feel more tender in your mouth. Also, don't saw at the meat too much; instead let the knife do the work.

You want the meat to be stable on your chopping board, particularly if it's a big joint. Place a dry napkin or piece of kitchen roll under the meat and a damp piece under the board to stop them both from sliding about.

A carving fork helps to secure the meat and keeps your fingers away from the sharp end. If you've not got these, then use kitchen tongs. It's best to transfer your slices of beef to a warm serving plate; this will stop them going cold.

BEEF ON THE BONE: FORE RIB, SIRLOIN
Start by cutting and removing any string holding the joint together. Then use your knife to cut down between the row of rib and the meat, and remove the bones. (The meat between them is delicious; remove that and save the bones themselves for the stockpot.) Underneath the meat there may be another thin piece of bone – remove this also. Then cut off thin slices and transfer them onto a warm plate. As you reach the end of the joint, keeping it upright becomes tricky, so turn flat-side-down and slice into smaller pieces that way.

BONELESS BEEF JOINTS: FILLET, RUMP, SILVERSIDE
Silverside, rump and mini roasting joints can all be treated in a similar fashion to beef on the bone and are easy to carve. Again, go with the grain and aim for thin, even slices.

SLOW-ROASTED JOINTS
Joints best suited for braising, such as thick flank, topside and rolled cap, can be sliced more thickly than roast beef, as they will be tenderer and have a looser texture.

A guide to steaks

A good steak is a thing of utter beauty; if done right, a charred crust should give way to a juicy, but not wet, interior. There are a range of steaks on the animal, each having a different size, shape, flavour and cooking method.

Not only that, but different steaks have different names in different countries. I've included a few other names should you find yourself in a steak house on holiday. Here are some popular and lesser known, but just as tasty steaks:

RIBEYE
Unsurprisingly, this comes from the rib section in the middle of the animal and has a good amount of fat in and around it. Traditionally, it was served off the bone, but like many steaks, you now see 'bone on' versions. Known as 'Scotch fillet' in Australia.

SIRLOIN
The many-named steak. Firstly, the word sirloin comes from the French for 'above the loin' – it's nothing to do with a King knighting a bit of meat. In modern French it's known as *aloyau* or *faux-filet*, while in the USA it's called 'New York Strip'. Like ribeye, many butchers now offer this 'bone on'.

RUMP
Fantastic steak that's cheaper than sirloin and can, if kept and matured well, have more flavour. As you'd expect, it comes from the rump or rear of the animal. Ideally, you want a thick version, 5cm+.

FILLET STEAK
From the bit of the animal that does no work, so is very tender – you can cut it with a spoon – but it can lack flavour. Best cooked quickly. Good for those who don't like to chew too much.

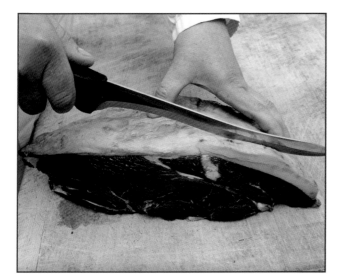

T-BONE / PORTERHOUSE
A T-bone comes from the lower middle area, and comprises a sirloin on one side, and a piece of fillet on the other. If the fillet side is small it's a T-bone, whereas if it's large it's a porterhouse. It takes skill to cook, however, as you don't want to overcook the fillet. A good-sized porterhouse is a great 'his and hers' or 'family' steak. With practice, you can get the fillet medium rare and the sirloin rare, which is just how I do it for my family.

FLAT IRON STEAK
The new kid on the block, this steak comes from the chuck at the front of the animal and was developed (or rediscovered?) by the Universities of Nebraska and Florida in 2002. They were looking at finding new steaks on the animal. It's best cooked rare and has a feather-like texture. Strangely, it's sometimes known as the Butler's steak in the UK, and the Oyster steak in Australia.

FEATHER BLADE STEAK
Both the flat iron and feather blade come from the same piece of meat. This cut has a large, tough piece of gristle running through the centre of it. Filleting it off (like skinning a salmon) gives you the flat iron, but cutting it across gives you a feather blade steak. You can cook them as is, but the connective tissue will remain; however, if you braise them it does start to break down.

HANGER STEAK OR ONGLET
The steak of choice for your classic French bistro. Big on flavour and taste, but best served rare or medium-rare at a push, otherwise it can toughen up.

BAVETTE
This steak is technically considered offal, as it comes from the abdominal muscles. Also known as skirt or goose skirt in the UK.

PICANHA
Pronounced 'pick-ann-yet', this steak-cum-joint is found in Brazil's many steak houses where it is revered. It's just becoming available in supermarkets, or you could ask your butcher to cut you one; they may need some notice, mind.

FRYING OR MINUTE STEAK
Can be cut from a variety of muscles, but more often than not comes from the thick flank on the hind legs. Its main attribute – besides its cheapness – is that it's very thin and cooks quickly over a hot flame. This makes it better suited for baguettes and sandwiches.

How to cook steak

There are plenty of different ways to cook a steak. There is even a multi-step process I found online that calls for your steak to be scored, seasoned, frozen, fried, roasted, basted, rested, roasted again, rested again and fried again. Apparently the results are phenomenal; however, it's perhaps not an everyday task.

There's no 100% right way to cook steak. What there is, though, is a few pieces of advice that I've found improve the end result.

SIZE
Thicker steaks are better than thin ones, so buy something around 3–5cm. This thickness allows a good crust and colour to form on

the outside of the steak, without drying out the inside. It's better to share a thicker steak between two than have two thin ones. Needless to say you want something dry aged.

TEMPERATURE
You'll often see advice such as 'let your meat come up to room temperature before cooking it'. Okay, but let's think about what this actually means. Room temperature is defined as around 20°C. My fridge is around 3°C. For the internal temperature of a large cut of meat to climb 17°C is going to take a lot longer than the often commanded 20 minutes – you're looking at over an hour. The phrase has almost become a shorthand for 'get things ready'. Of course a quick search online reveals plenty of people who think it makes little difference to the final result. After all, a few seconds on the griddle will raise the internal temperature as much as hours on the counter. Actually temperature is secondary to the next important attribute…

DRYNESS
Even dry-aged beef will still have plenty of moisture present on its surface. This is the death of a good steak, as it will boil instead of char when it hits the hot pan. Consequently you want to remove as much of this as possible using kitchen roll.

SEASONING
Another key thing is seasoning, you need to use top-quality sea salt and season the steak well. You can do this prior to cooking; the salt will help form a good crust during cooking. I don't season with pepper until on the plate; indeed, sometimes I omit it entirely.

COOKING METHOD
Cooking a steak on a griddle pan or in a frying pan is different from cooking over coals. Coals get much hotter, and can cook much quicker. If indoors, don't think of it as cooking a steak, think of it as a monthly test of the smoke alarm, because to cook a steak properly indoors, you're going to want to have the windows open and the extractor fan on the highest setting – there will be smoke!

TURNING
Restaurants and steak houses like the grid-iron look, two sets of black strips at 45° to each other. If you're using a griddle pan, repeated turning can leave you with lots of lines, which you might not want. I tend to turn once, but if I'm cooking on a flat rather than ridged cast-iron trivet, I'll flip more frequently.

1 Dry the surface of the steak with kitchen paper, and season very well.

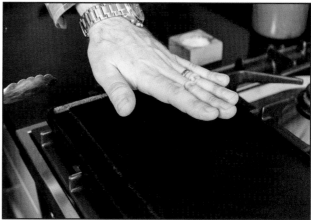

2 Get your pan smoking hot; do not use any oil.

3 Using tongs, place any fat on the steak in the pan first and let a little fat render out.

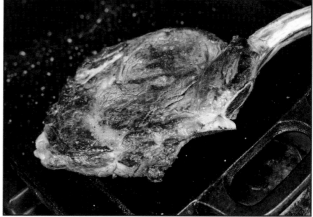

4 Place the steak flat-side-down onto the pan and let it cook for a couple of minutes. Don't move it. It's ready to turn when it comes away easily from the pan.

5 Flip over and cook the other side for the same amount of time as the first, then flip back (adjusting the angle if you want the grid effect) and flip a final time. These last two flips should be less than a minute.

6 Let the steak rest somewhere warm for 5–10 minutes, preferably on a rack. Cut and serve on a board.

Note: you can 'dress' the steak towards the end of cooking by adding a tablespoon of butter and letting it foam up.

Sous vide and other ways of cooking

Sous vide (French for 'under vacuum') is the process of sealing food in a plastic bag and then cooking it very gently in warm water. The bag helps to contain any juices and the gentle heat penetrates the meat, cooking it evenly without drying it out. Because the temperature is much lower, the cells in the meat do not burst; also the steak cooks evenly throughout. Of course a downside is that you need either a dedicated sous vide machine, or one of the new stick device versions. It also takes a lot more total cooking time too, but if you're into cooking steaks in new and exciting ways, try it.

All the rage in chef circles a few years ago and heralded by the great Heston himself as the future of cooking, it is especially good for cooking meat. However, there are detractors, particularly in the US, who think it results in a tender but slightly flavourless result. Many people like the reliability, consistency, and quality of using a sous vide machine, which is why they first appeared in the restaurant trade.

PRE- OR POST- SEAR A SOUS VIDE STEAK?

As you'd expect, there's advocates of both searing the meat in a pan *before* placing in the water, and those who prefer to sear it afterwards. I think that if you've not got a proper vacuum packer and sous vide machine and are 'hacking something together', pre-searing is the way to go. That way, you know any bacteria on the outside of your meat are well and truly toast. You can even do this with a blowtorch!

STEAKS

Steaks are often one of the first things people try when they cook sous vide. The aim is to ensure that your steak is cooked evenly throughout the meat, from the centre to the edge, but crucially not overdone. Most guides recommend a temperature of 58°C for around 90 minutes to produce a steak that is medium rare. Obviously, you still need to sear it in a screaming hot pan to produce a good crust.

Thickness matters when it comes to cooking steaks in this way; whatever cut you choose, it's much more likely to work if it's 3–4cm thick. Any less than that and you'll overcook the inside when finishing it off in the pan.

OTHER CUTS AND MEATS

Cheaper cuts with lots of interconnecting tissue that needs to be broken down can also be cooked sous vide, however they'll need a much longer cooking time. Cuts like ribs or brisket can be cooked for as long as 16 hours, and often up to 48 hours.

Pork and chicken can both be cooked sous vide. Again, you want to make sure they're cooked thoroughly, so use your meat thermometer.

Finally, you can apparently cook fish, vegetables and eggs sous vide, but that's way out of the scope of this book.

RISE OF THE MACHINES

A few years ago, sous vide machines cost hundreds of pounds. Now the price has fallen to something that, while not cheap, is at least affordable to the dedicated home cook. The question you've got to ask yourself is, 'am I really going to use it?' But hey, that applies to most things in life!

Of course, necessity is the mother of invention and the Internet is home to many 'how to build a cheap sous vide machine' tutorials. I own a vacuum packer, and have experimented with sealing steaks in bags and using my meat thermometer, gently cooking. I'd say this: it's very easy to overdo it with this approach. If you've not got a vacuum packer, one online tutorial advocates placing steaks in a ziplock bag and placing it in a cool box filled with warm water for an hour before flash-frying the steak. This might produce a result, but it's pretty unscientific and not very controllable.

The point is there are many ways to cook a steak; sous vide is just one approach. Like all meat cookery, keep things neat and tidy and plan what you're doing properly, and you'll be fine.

THE TOM KERRIDGE METHOD

Tom Kerridge once cooked me one of the best T-bone steaks I have ever eaten, and he did it three times in one day. We were doing a series of demonstrations at *The Ideal Home Show* and Tom's method is kind of like a simple sous vide. Here's what he did: take a really good, thick T-bone and place it in a dish, in the oven, for around four hours at 50°C (not a fan oven; it'll dry it out). Then all you need to do is colour and crust up the exterior in a hot pan with some foaming butter. This is the steak to serve to people who don't like rare steak. The inside sort of cooks, but doesn't dry out and still remains juicy. It needs to be a big cut, and a very low oven, but it's an interesting technique.

Classic roast rib of beef

This is it, the big one. Actually, despite being the most costly ingredient in this book, it's surprisingly easy to cook. There's very little faffing, prep or intricate techniques involved. All you need is a trivet of vegetables underneath to help make gravy, a meat thermometer and salt and pepper.

The four-ribbed joint pictured here and on the cover of this book weighed around 3kg and would easily serve 8–10, with all the trimmings. It sat on a trivet of vegetables in my fan oven at 250°C for 20 minutes then down to 150°C for about 100 minutes.

I then let it rest for ages – over 40 minutes – during which it was still cooking. In fact, if you insert a meat thermometer into the thickest part of a joint straight out of the oven and record the temperature, it will actually rise as the meat rests and sucks heat back into the centre.

Remember, if your meat's too rare, you can always put it back in the oven, if it's overdone, it's ruined.

INGREDIENTS
- 4 carrots, chopped
- 2 sticks of celery, chopped
- 5 small onions, halved
- 1 head of garlic, halved (optional)
- 2 tablespoons of oil
- 1 flower of star anise (optional)
- 1 four-rib, on-the-bone joint of beef
- 1 tablespoon of water

METHOD
Place the vegetables, oil and star anise in the bottom of a roasting dish. Ensure the onions are flat-side-up to support the meat, or alternatively use a rack to lift the meat up off the dish. This allows heat to penetrate all around the meat.

BEEF COOKING TIMES

To be honest, these are a bit of a rule of thumb. Your oven will cook differently to mine, and something like an Aga is different still. Heat the oven to 230°C and roast for 20 minutes, and then roast for 12–15 minutes per 450g for rare, 20 minutes per 450g for medium and 25 minutes for well done. This is just a guide, however; a joint taken straight from the fridge and cooked in a non-fan oven will behave totally differently.

If you have people who like beef more 'done' than that, give them slices from the end of the joint, keeping the middle for yourself. Cooked beef, even cooked rare, is a bright, juicy pink; if the centre of your joint is a deep red and still lukewarm to the touch, it's not quite cooked enough. On the other hand, if it's a uniform brown or grey throughout, it's overcooked.

Perhaps a better method is to use your thermometer and aim for an internal temperature of around 55–60°C in the thickest part of the meat. Resting time is crucial: remember meat stays hot, or at least still warm, long after vegetables and even potatoes have gone stone cold.

Internal beef temperature guide:
Rare 60°C   Medium 65°C   Well done 75°C

How to make beef burgers

Nothing encapsulates the 'dude food' movement more than the recent rise of the burger. For years in Britain, it was just seen as fast food – junk food almost. Then people realised that when you made them properly, they were actually quite nice. Now you can throw a stick in many of our cities and hit a tattooed bloke selling burgers washed down with craft beer. What accounts for their success? Well they're easy to make, fairly cheap and pretty much everyone likes them.

Once you've made your own patties, you'll never go back to the tasteless, oddly textured ones you see in the shops.

THE MEAT

The cut I like to use is chuck. It has a good fat-to-meat ratio, which is key to keeping a burger juicy. If your chuck is coming up a little lean, you can cut the chuck with something like short rib. Don't waste money on wagyu beef, fillet or sirloin – they're much better as steaks – making a burger from these cuts is like doing a milk round in an Aston Martin.

EXTRAS

No, not needed. You're just diluting the end product. Egg, breadcrumbs, onion and such may help bind, but I think ruin the meaty flavour and open texture of a good burger. In the past they were added because: a) us Brits didn't really know what we were doing, b) burger presses weren't as available and c) bread's cheaper than meat so makes it go further (by giving you less of it).

Also it's 'no' to other flavourings, such as sun-dried tomato, garlic or cheese. You want meat, mate, and by meat I mean beef. If you're going to mince lamb, make kofta; if you're going to mince pork, make scotch eggs or sausages.

GRINDING

Grinding your own meat makes you a real pro: once you've ground, pressed and cooked your own burgers you won't go back. It's one of the easiest parts of food prep that delivers a noticeable leap in quality, taste and flavour.

I've got an electric meat grinder that I bought for under £50. Indeed, many are now around the £30 mark, while hand-cranked, tabletop ones are cheaper still. Also, if you've already got a stand mixer, like a Kenwood K Mix, you can buy a meat grinder attachment for it. Many meat grinders also come with bits that allow you to make sausages, too, so if you're serious about meat (and I hope you are, that's why you're reading this book), I'd seriously consider getting one.

How to grind meat

1 Keep everything as cold as possible. Dice the meat into cubes, place in a large bowl and put that and the grinder attachments in the freezer for 30 minutes to chill right down. Put your burger press in there, too. The colder the meat is the firmer it'll be, meaning it will 'cut' better when it hits the plate. If it's warm and flaccid, it'll just smear and stretch rather than cut. Keeping everything cold helps with hygiene too.

2 Add the diced meat to the grinder and press down firmly. Needless to say, be careful of long hair, loose clothing and your fingers. Most grinders come with two plates, coarse and fine. I like to grind on the coarse plate. There are some that believe if you're going to cook your burgers over flame, use the fine plate, as the coarse one can let too much of the fat drain away.

3 Season the ground meat with salt and pepper. Now's also the time to add any other flavourings.

4 Take a handful, about 170g, and place in your burger press. Many come with wax paper circles but I don't bother using them. Press lightly: you don't want to force your burger too much, you just want to ensure that it stays together during the cooking process. You can put these back in the fridge for a while now if you like.

CLEANING TIP
To get the last of the meat out of the grinder, place chunks of sliced white bread in, this will force it out. Grind this into a separate bowl, though.

NOT GOT A GRINDER?
No problem. If you don't own a meat grinder get coarse-cut mince from your butcher. Don't buy that thin, straggly red mince you see in supermarkets, it's good for nothing.

How to cook beef burgers

So, you've made your own burgers from scratch – excellent. Now you're ready to cook them. Apart from a few balmy days in summer when you can get the grill out, I imagine most of you will be cooking on the hob. I like to get all the other things ready first, before I start cooking the burgers.

INGREDIENTS

To make approx. 4 burgers

- Around 700g coarse ground beef
- Sea salt, to season
- 4 slices of cheddar cheese
- 4 brioche buns
- Your favourite sauce
- 1 beef tomato, thinly sliced
- 4 leaves of either little gem or round lettuce
- 4 pickles
- 4 slices of thinly sliced onion

METHOD

1 Firstly, you need a good, heavy cast-iron pan or even better, a griddle plate placed directly over the burners. Slice the buns, and toast lightly on the griddle for no more than a few minutes as it warms up. Toasting the buns stops them going soggy. Brush away any crumbs that fall off the buns, as these will burn.

2 Get the griddle really hot. Season your burgers with a good amount of sea salt just before you're about to cook them.

3 Place on the hot griddle and do not touch it for 4 minutes. Don't keep pressing it down; it may be satisfying to hear that sizzle, but all you're doing is squeezing the 'juiciness' out of the meat and onto the plate.

4 Season the side facing up, flip your burger once and let this side cook for around 3 minutes. If you're going for cheese, now's the time to add it to the cooked side facing up. Once cooked turn out the heat and move the burgers to the edge of the griddle plate, or remove from the griddle pan and let them rest for a moment while you assemble the buns and toppings.

BURGER STRUCTURE

What's the correct way to layer a burger? Any way you like! However, here's my way: bottom of the bun, sauce, meat, cheese, tomato, lettuce, pickles, onion, more sauce spread on the top half of the bun. Putting the 'veg' on top of the meat helps keep things stable. Lettuce under a burger is liable to slide around, in my experience.

A SHORT HISTORY OF THE BEEF BURGER IN BRITAIN

Eddie Gold opened the first branch of Wimpy in the Lyon's Tea Room, Piccadilly in 1954. There you got a burger on a plate, with a knife and fork. McDonald's, meanwhile, arrived in Britain in 1974, with their first store in Woolwich, south London, and Burger King a few years later in 1977. And that's how it stayed by and large until the post-crash burger big bang of 2009, led by the likes of Meatliquor and others. Many have now gone on from street food trucks and pop-ups to actual bricks and mortar restaurants. Another change is the size of the burgers. They've tripled in size since those original 1950s ones, piling on the grams from an easily manageable 110g to a massive 340g today. Some are now over 20cm high!

Burger buns

So, there's no point going to all the effort of hand-making beautiful burgers and then slinging your meat on any old floury bap. No, if you're going to do it properly, it's got to be on brioche buns.

While I have occasionally seen these in supermarkets and at my local bakers, they're not that widely available. Thankfully they're not that hard to make either. This recipe makes around a dozen delicious buns.

Traditional brioche – a breakfast bread – is heavily enriched with egg and butter, giving a bright golden colour. For brioche burger buns, however, we don't want too much butter, as this can cause a soggy bottom when your hot burger hits the bread.

INGREDIENTS

For the brioche buns
- 3 medium eggs
- 70ml warm milk
- 30g caster sugar
- 2 teaspoons of dried instant yeast
- 5g salt
- 300g strong bread flour
- 100g butter, cut into cubes at room temperature
- 1 tablespoon of vegetable oil

For the egg wash
- 1 egg, beaten
- 40ml milk
- Sesame seed, to sprinkle (optional)

METHOD

1 In a stand mixer fitted with a dough hook, place the egg, milk, sugar and yeast. Mix on a low speed until it's well mixed and the sugar dissolves.
2 Add the salt and the flour in small amounts.
3 Once it's all in and combined, add the butter and keep mixing for around 20 minutes until the dough comes cleanly away from the sides of the bowl and it's light and elastic.
4 Add a little vegetable oil to a clean bowl and transfer the dough to it. Cover with cling film and leave to prove for 1–3 hours, depending on how warm your kitchen is.
5 Once proved, knock the dough back and knead by hand again for a few minutes. Roll out into a sausage and, using scissors, cut in half, then each half in half, then each of those four pieces into three – these will be your buns.

SHAPING THE BUNS

6 There's a bit of a knack to doing this; slightly flatten each piece and then fold the edges into the centre. Turn the dough over, so the seam is on the underside, and give a little roll around to even out. You want 12 nicely shaped balls of dough, around 80g in weight. Transfer to a baking tray lined with baking parchment and cover with a piece of lightly oiled cling film. Leave for another hour or so to prove again.
7 Heat the oven to 180°C and place a small baking tray filled with a little water in the bottom of the oven.
8 Just before placing the buns in the oven, make the egg wash by combining the egg and milk, then use a pastry brush to lightly cover the top of each bun. This would be the time to add any sesame seeds if you want that look. Place in the oven for about 15 minutes. You can do all this the day before your barbecue; just keep the buns in an air-tight container.

Beef stew and dumplings

Warming, hearty, filling – beef stew is comfort personified. It's one of what I call 'fry and forget' recipes, as you just have to brown the beef and vegetables, add the liquids, and forget about it for a couple of hours. The oven does most of the work.

INGREDIENTS
Serves 4–6
For the stew
- 2 large onions (or 4 medium ones)
- 3 large carrots
- 1kg skirt steak
- 3 tablespoons of seasoned flour
- 1 tablespoon of beef dripping or lard (or vegetable oil, if you must)
- 1 bottle (around 300ml) of porter, stout or dark ale
- 1 single petal from a 'flower' of star anise
- Salt and pepper, to season
- Beef shin bone or any other bones

For the dumplings
- 400g self-raising flour
- Pinch of salt
- 200g beef suet
- Approx. 150ml water

I really like using skirt steak in stews. It's cheap and flavourful, and can take the long, slow cooking stews really need. Cheek is good too. Critical, I think, to many beef dishes is star anise. It adds a subtle perfumed flavour that offsets the richness of the beef.

METHOD
1 Peel and chop all the onions and carrots, the latter into large pieces.
2 Chop the skirt into strips along the grain on the meat, and then into 'domino'-sized pieces. Tip the flour onto a plate and dust the meat with it.
3 Heat the fat in a large casserole and add the meat in small batches so that the pieces don't touch each other. Don't move it around. After a few minutes, try to pick a piece up with your tongs. When it has a good crust on it, the meat should come away easily; if it sticks to the pan, it's not ready yet.
4 Once both sides of the meat are brown, remove to a clean plate and brown the rest of the meat.
5 When that's done, add a little more fat, the vegetables and then the beer, scraping all the little bits off the bottom of the pan with a spoon. Add the bones, if using, followed by the star anise and pepper (add the salt at the end of cooking).
6 Add the meat back into the pan and cover with a cartouche (see page 23). Place in a 150ºC oven for 3 hours, checking occasionally.
7 After 2 hours, make the dumplings. Sieve the flour and salt into a bowl, add the suet and combine thoroughly.
8 Make a well in the centre and add small amounts of water – enough to bring it together

as loose dough. Slowly bring the dough together with a spoon until you can get your hands in. It's ready when it's not too wet and no flour remains in the bowl. You might need to add a little extra water.
9 Chill the dumpling mixture for 15 minutes before using.
10 Roll into small balls, about the size of golf balls (they will expand a little during cooking). Remove the bones now – they've done their work – and tuck the dumplings into the stew for the last half hour of cooking time, where they'll bob about in the meaty juices getting all nice and soggy underneath, while crisping up on top. Serve with mash and peas.

Shin of beef ragu

The shin spends its time supporting all the other bits of the rather-heavy cow as it waddles around the field. Consequently, it's a tough, hardworking muscle that needs long, slow cooking. This dish does just that – it's the sort of thing you put on at 9am for dinner that evening. It's 'spag bog' with gold-plated, turned-up-to-11 knobs on; even the pasta is bigger and better. Make sure you serve in warmed bowls, with plenty of grated Parmesan and a thumping red wine.

You'll need a 2kg shin of beef with the bone in. Either ask your butcher to cut it into a few 5cm+ 'steaks' (similar to osso buco), or cut it yourself with a saw. I think the marrow in the bone is critical for getting that rich, shiny, beefy flavour.

INGREDIENTS
Serves 4–6
- 3 onions, peeled and chopped
- 3 carrots, peeled and diced
- 3 cloves of garlic, crushed
- 2 sticks of celery, diced
- Glug of sunflower, olive or vegetable oil
- 500ml red wine
- 3 tins of whole plum tomatoes
- Salt and pepper, to season
- 1 teaspoon of oregano
- 1 tablespoon of flour
- 2kg thickly sliced beef shin, bone in
- Knob of butter

To serve
- 500g pappardelle
- Grated parmesan cheese

TOP TOMATOES

Always buy whole plum tomatoes, rather than chopped, as they have less water. I also like to cut off the little top bit you get on each one, as it doesn't break down as well during cooking.

METHOD
1 Peel and chop the vegetables and add to a large pan with a glug of oil. Put on a gentle heat and soften the vegetables. When the onion has gone translucent, add the wine and the plum tomatoes. Season and add the oregano.
2 Tip the flour onto a plate and season, then dust the shin slices in it. Heat a knob of butter in a separate frying pan and, when foaming, add the shin slices. Colour the shin briefly on each side and then transfer to the tomato and vegetable mixture, along with any scrapings from the pan. Make a cartouche (see page 23) and place in the oven at 120ºC for four hours.
3 Four hours later… Remove from the oven and use a slotted spoon to carefully remove the beef shins. Shred with two forks on a chopping board.
4 Using a stick blender, blitz the remaining tomato sauce before returning the beef to the pan and combining (you can do all this a day in advance and leave to cool).
5 Big, thick ribbons of pappardelle work best with this dish. Cook following the packet instructions and drain. Spoon the ragu into the pasta pan, combine and serve with the Parmesan.

Cornish pasties

This recipe comes from the body charged with protecting the production of Cornish pasties: the Cornish Pasty Association. You can rest assured it's the 'proper job'.

INGREDIENTS

To make 4 pasties
For shortcrust pastry (rough puff can also be used):
- 120g lard or white shortening
- 125g butter
- 500g strong bread flour (it's important to use a stronger flour than normal as you need the extra strength in the gluten to produce strong, pliable pastry)
- 175ml cold water
- 1 teaspoon of salt

For the filling
- 450g good quality beef skirt, cut into cubes
- 450g potato, diced
- 250g swede, diced
- 200g onion, sliced
- Salt and pepper, to taste
- 1 beaten egg with milk (optional), to glaze

METHOD

1. Rub the two types of fat lightly into the flour until it resembles breadcrumbs.
2. Add the salt and the water, then bring the mixture together and knead until the pastry becomes elastic. This will take longer than normal pastry, but it gives the pastry the strength that is needed to hold the filling and retain a good shape. This can also be done in a food mixer.
3. Cover with cling film and leave to rest for 3 hours in the fridge. This is a very important stage, as it's almost impossible to roll and shape the pastry when it's fresh.
4. Roll out the pastry and cut into circles, approximately 20cm in diameter. A side plate is an ideal size to use as a guide.
5. Layer the vegetables and meat on top of the pastry, adding plenty of seasoning. Bring the pastry around and crimp the edges together (see our guide to crimping below). Glaze with a beaten egg, or an egg and milk mixture.
6. Bake at 165°C for about 40–45 minutes until golden.

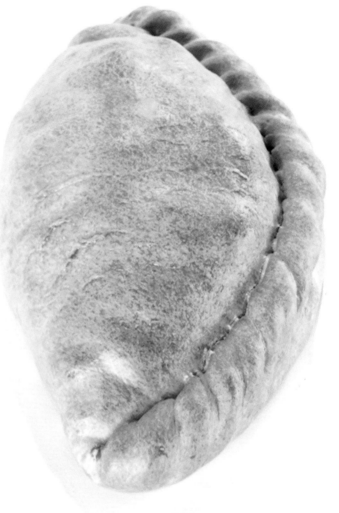

HOW TO CRIMP

Crimping is one of the secrets to a true Cornish pasty. A good hand crimp is usually a sign of a good handmade pasty. To crimp a Cornish pasty:
1. Lightly brush the edge of the pastry base with water.
2. Fold the other half of the pastry over the filling and squeeze the half.
3. Push down on the edge of the pasty and, using your index finger and thumb, twist the edge of the pastry over to form a crimp.
4. Repeat this process along the edge of the pasty.
5. When you've crimped along the edge, tuck the end corners underneath.

Bresaola and cured beef

While many other cured meats are made from pork, bresaola – a speciality of the Lombardy area of Italy – is made with beef. The aromatics used are juniper and rosemary, while the cut of beef is made from the tender and lean top (or inside) round, found on the rear of the animal.

INGREDIENTS

- 1 round cut of beef
- 1 tablespoon of ground rosemary
- 1 tablespoon of ground juniper
- 1 packet of Prague Powder #2
- Around 100g salt
- Around 100g sugar
- 1 teaspoon of black pepper

If you're interested in having a go at making one, it's one of the simplest bits of charcuterie you can do. You'll need Prague Powder #2 (this is different from the #1 powder used in making bacon and is especially designed for air-dried charcuterie). This cure is a mixture of three forms of Sodium: Sodium Chloride (more commonly know as salt), Sodium Nitrite and Sodium Nitrate – consequently be careful with it. You can order it easily online from http://www.sausagemaking.org, and you will find lots of information there, too.

The amount of cure depends on how big your meat is. A rough guide is 2.5g of #2 powder per kg of meat (in addition to extra salt), but follow the advice on the packet.

METHOD

1. Ask your butcher for the top round cut (you can also use the fillet, but that's way more expensive and you risk ruining it).
2. Remove any outside membrane or sinew (don't worry about the piece in the middle).
3. Grind your aromatics and make up the cure according to the packet's instructions based on the weight of your *trimmed* meat. Set half of it aside in a sealed container.
4. Put the other half in the ziplock bag and add the beef. Massage well and place in the fridge for a week, turning daily.
5. After a week remove the beef, wipe off any remaining cure and fluid, and place the meat in a clean ziplock bag with the other half of the cure. Return to the fridge for another week, again turning daily.
6. After the second week, remove and wipe clean again. Weigh the meat and make a note of how much it weighs.
7. You can now wrap it in muslin, truss it up using butcher's string and hang it somewhere cool, dry and not too humid, such as in a garage. Weigh it every few days: it should be 'done' when the weight has shrunk by 30% – this should take around 3–4 weeks.
8. A white bloom of mould on the outside is okay. You can wipe this off with kitchen paper soaked in white wine vinegar.

Meatballs

Nearly every country in the world has a meatball dish, from Chinese 'wanzi', made with steamed pork, to the fried versions found in Scandinavia and served with loganberry jam.

The beauty of meatballs is that you can customise them to fit the ingredients you've got in. Here are some of the variables you can play with: meat, additions, sauces and size.

MEAT

This can include minced pork, beef, lamb, venison and even chicken (Matzo anyone?). Drier meats such as beef and venison benefit from a small inclusion of pork to help keep them moist. This can take the form of pork mince or even a de-skinned sausage or two.

ADDITIONS

Here you can add whatever you like, such as crushed fennel seeds, chilli flakes, garlic, onions, feta cheese, Parmesan, breadcrumbs, eggs, ground nuts, parsley, mint, oregano and thyme.

If you're adding lots of extras like herbs then you'll need to also add a beaten egg to help bind the mixture together. Soaking the bread in milk first is also an option.

You can also experiment with adding a 'crust' to your meatballs by rolling them in a mixture of flour with a teaspoon of mustard powder.

SAUCES

Meatballs generally need a little sauce to help them along. The most obvious choices are the classic tomato, or a creamier mushroomed version. Once fried, you can also add them to soups and broths.

SIZE

Meatballs for soups should be small, about the size of a £2 coin. If you're having them with pasta, you can make them bigger – say the size of a ping pong ball up to a golf ball. Whichever size you make, consistency is the key. That way they'll all cook at the same time. The best way to do this is to weigh the mixture each time, unless you're confident judging by eye.

Basic meatball recipe

The 'vanilla' of the meatball world and a good basic recipe that's fine on its own or as a base for other flavours.

INGREDIENTS

Serves 4–6

- 500g minced beef
- 200g pork (or plain sausage meat)
- 1 egg
- 2 teaspoons of dried oregano
- 2 teaspoons of thyme
- Plenty of salt and pepper
- Glug of oil and knob of butter to fry them in

For the basic tomato sauce

- 1 onion
- 1 can of plum tomatoes or passata
- 1 pinch of salt
- 1 pinch of caster sugar
- Torn basil and grated Parmesan, to serve

METHOD

1 Thoroughly combine all the ingredients in a large bowl.
2 Using kitchen scales, portion into equally sized amounts, around 30–50g.
3 Wet your hands and squash each portion together in your hands before rolling in a circular fashion to make a ball. Repeat using the rest of the mixture.
4 Add 2 tablespoons of oil and a knob of butter to a large, non-stick pan and then add the meatballs in batches. Swill the pan around to encourage the meatballs to roll around and colour on all sides. Repeat until all the meatballs are cooked.
5 For the tomato sauce, add a chopped onion to the same pan used to brown the meatballs and gently cook until soft.
6 Add a carton of passata or a can of plum tomatoes and cook on a high heat until the sauce has reduced.
7 Season with salt, pepper and a pinch of caster sugar. Return the meatballs to the pan and cook for a further 10–15 minutes. Sprinkle over grated Parmesan cheese and some torn basil, and serve with pasta.

Other cooking methods

For a softer result, which is good for delicate meats such as veal, you can 'poach' the raw meatballs in the sauce. You can also bake the meatballs on a baking tray in a 180°C oven for around 30–40 minutes. Ca' d'Oro Alla Vedova, a small tavern in Venice, sells deep fried pork and veal meatballs.

Beef Wellington

A beef Wellington is certainly a stunning dish and a great showpiece to put on the table. It's quite technical to make, and not cheap either, as it uses fillet steak; but pull this off, and no one will ever doubt your kitchen credentials again.

You'll see all over the Internet that it's named after Arthur Wellesley, the first Duke of Wellington (1769–1852) – it isn't. Nor is it anything to do with Wellington, New Zealand, or wellington boots. Indeed the recipe doesn't appear in any English cookbook until the 1970s, though the *Oxford English Dictionary* has a reference from a restaurant in New York in the 1930s. It is, in fact, just a classic *filet de bœuf en croûte*. It's important to serve it with a wine-based sauce.

INGREDIENTS

Serves 6–8

- 800g–1kg fillet of beef
- Glug of vegetable or sunflower oil
- 2 cloves of garlic, finely chopped
- 2 shallots, finely chopped
- 400g chestnut mushrooms, finely chopped
- A few dried porcini mushrooms, rehydrated
- Small bunch of parsley, finely chopped
- 2 tablespoons of double cream
- 100g smooth pâté
- 4–5 ready-made pancakes
- 1–2 packets of ready-rolled all-butter puff pastry (have a spare, just in case)
- 1 egg beaten with a dash of milk (to glaze and seal)

METHOD

1 First, sear the beef – a mini project in itself, this. Get a pan as hot as you can and add the oil. When the oil starts to shimmer, add the beef fillet and gently roll it around to colour on all sides. You want the beef to be cooked on the outside, but still pink in the middle – this will vary depending on the thickness of your fillet. Also you can't really tell unless you cut it open. Generally I've found it takes longer than you think, and a medium Wellington is better than one that oozes blood everywhere! Alternatively, you can roast the fillet in a 230ºC oven for around 15 minutes. The reason for doing this is that when the completed Wellington goes into the oven, it's only to cook the pastry. There's not really time to cook the fillet further. Once you've done that, leave it to cool.

2 Next make the duxelles: this is basically a mushroom paste that provides extra flavour. You can either finely chop the garlic, shallots, chestnut mushrooms and porcini mushrooms by hand, or blitz the whole lot up in a food processor.

3 Once you've got your minced mushrooms and shallots, fry them in a little vegetable or sunflower oil until soft, drain off any liquid, and add the cream and the parsley. Cook for a further 10 minutes until the pan is quite dry, then leave to cool. When cold, mix with the pâté.

Assembling

4 Lay a piece of foil on the work surface and place 3 or 4 pancakes, overlapped in a row slightly longer than the length of the beef fillet. Spread on the cooked mushroom mixture. Place the cooked, cooled fillet on top and fold over the pancakes to cover the fillet. Trim off any bits that cause you trouble. Use the foil to help you shape the pancake around the beef. Don't press too hard, or your mushroom mixture will ooze out.

5 Unfurl the puff pastry and place the pancake-wrapped fillet in the centre. Fold the edges over and seal the edges with egg wash.

6 Place back on the foil and chill for 20 minutes while the oven gets hot. Heat the oven to 220ºC and put your baking tray in.

7 Place the Wellington with the sealed edges down, brush with the remaining egg wash, and place onto the hot baking tray. Cook for 25 minutes until the pastry is cooked and golden brown.

8 Leave to cool slightly before serving, cut into thick slices (start at the middle) and – with any luck – your beef fillet will be pink and juicy in the centre. If not, pop it back in the oven for 5 more minutes.

Cottage pie

Traditionally a use for leftover beef, but now often made with fresh mince, cottage pie first gets its mention in 1791 so predates the young shepherd's pie by some considerable years. Interestingly some recipes for cottage (and indeed shepherd's) pie call for a layer of potato *underneath* the filling as well as on top.

Today, the recipes for both pies are similar in ingredients, bar the change of meat. However, I think a good cottage pie should include things that improve beef's robustness; consequently I add beer to the filling and a spoon of grated horseradish to the mash. I'm not a big fan of adding tinned tomatoes to cottage pie filling, I think it turns it into something more like a Bolognese sauce. Instead, use good quality meat, stock and beer to give maximum flavour.

INGREDIENTS
Serves 4, fills a medium to large pie dish
For the filling
- 1 large onion, diced
- 2–3 medium carrots, diced into cubes
- 1 stick of celery, diced
- ½ tablespoon of sunflower oil
- 500g beef mince (or you could use shin of beef chopped finely with a knife)
- 200ml beef stock
- 300ml ale or beer
- ½ teaspoon of dried thyme
- 1 teaspoon of tomato puree
- ½ teaspoon of cornflour
- A large dash of Worcestershire sauce
- Salt and pepper, to season

For the topping
- 1kg potatoes, cut into chunks
- 90g butter
- Splash of milk
- Teaspoon of horseradish (optional)

METHOD
1 Peel the carrot and onion and chop into a fine dice, along with the celery. Peel and cut up the potatoes. Bring a pan of water to the boil and add the potatoes.
2 Heat the oil in a frying pan on a high heat. Fry the beef mince in small batches and remove. Turn the heat down and fry the onion, carrot and celery in the pan until softened.
3 Return the mince and add the stock, beer, dried thyme and tomato puree. Mix the cornflour with a little water and add to thicken up the gravy a little. Add the Worcestershire sauce, and salt and pepper.
4 Simmer on a low heat for 30 minutes. (Sometimes I cook the filling in the oven; if you'd rather do this, pop it in for an hour at 130ºC.)
5 Meanwhile keep an eye on the spuds. It's very important to let them steam dry after draining off the water,

otherwise you'll have too wet a mash. Mash and add the butter, the milk and the horseradish sauce if using. The full recipe is on page 155.

Assembling
6 Remember to let your mashed potatoes and filling cool a little before putting the former on the latter. Start by applying little dollops of potato using a tablespoon, dotting them around on top of your filling. If you put the whole lot in, it'll sink like a bowling ball. Gradually add more dollops until they start to join together. Then, with the back of a spoon or a palette knife, smooth the potato together. Adding a layer of seasoned breadcrumbs over the mash turns a cottage pie into a Cumberland pie, apparently.
7 Place in a heated oven at 180ºC for 20 minutes until the potato is golden brown and the filling is hot.

Classic steak tartare

Meat, raw meat. However, despite the visceral sounding nature of this dish, it's actually quite sophisticated in its execution and construction. And if that wasn't enough, it's often served with a raw egg yolk. If you have a particularly annoying Paleo diet-following friend, serve them this.

Firstly, what it is not. The story that the Tartar people from the steppes of Asia would put raw meat under their saddle to tenderise after a day's riding is complete jabberwocky. Also, it is not just a 'raw hamburger' with a raw egg yolk on top.

What is it then? Well, a dish of the freshest, best quality fillet steak money can buy, served with a few punchy additional flavours. Indeed, it was once known as 'steak a la American', a name that caused many a US visitor to Europe to think they were on safe ground when touring Paris, only to be served raw meat.

Needless to say, cleanliness has never been closer to godliness when preparing this dish. You want a small amount of best quality, aged fillet steak.

I think it's best served as a starter, perhaps enough for two or three good mouthfuls, rather than as a main course. Some good bread or toast is a must too.

INGREDIENTS

Serves 2

- 200g best quality fillet steak
- 5 finely chopped cornichons
- 1 tablespoon of capers, finely chopped
- 1 tablespoon of parsley, finely chopped
- 1 tablespoon of Dijon or mild mustard
- A few dashes of Tabasco sauce
- A few dashes of Worcestershire sauce
- Lots of sea salt and black pepper
- 2 free-range egg yolks

METHOD

1 Place the fillet steak in the freezer to firm up, but not freeze solid – it'll make it easier to cut. I'd recommend using two chopping boards and a very sharp knife for this recipe: one to remove the outer layer of the steak and any potential dangers, and one to chop it finely on. (If you've only one, clean it thoroughly between stages. Clean the knife between stages too, obviously.)

2 Place the piece of fillet upright on board one and slice gently down, removing a thin outer layer around the circumference. Remove the top and bottom of it and transfer to the other board.

3 Wash your hands and the knife with hot soapy water, finely dice the remaining steak on a clean chopping board and place in a bowl. Add the cornichons, capers and parsley.

4 In a separate bowl mix together the mustard, tabasco and Worcestershire sauce and season very well. Mix into the meat and combine thoroughly.

5 Separate the egg yolks from the whites.

6 Using a biscuit cutter, make a disc of the meat on the plate. With a spoon, make a small indentation into the top and place the yolk in the impression. Serve at once.

Oven busters

Webb's *Third Law of Meat Price Dynamics* states that the cost of a specific cut rises as the number of chefs gussying it up and selling it increases, and I reckon beef ribs are going to go through what lamb shanks and pork belly have been through previously. Namely, you used to be able to get them a lot cheaper.

Short ribs, or Jacob's ladder as they are known in the UK, are big on beefy flavour. They can vary in size, but ask your butcher to cut them into square-ish pieces. There's a bone in there, to give structure, and plenty of connecting tissue, fat and tasty meat to give flavour.

The reason people haven't quite gone doolally for them yet is that you have to cook them low and slow, which rules out a 'just back from work' tea – unless, of course, you've figured out how to put your oven on a timer. So read the manual that came with the oven and get them while they're (comparatively) cheap.

Ideally, you want all the ribs in a single layer in a dish or tin, rather than on top of each other, so use either a wide, shallow casserole or seal the ribs in a frying pan before transferring to an ovenproof dish.

METHOD

1 Heat the oven to 130ºC.
2 Add some oil to an ovenproof casserole or roasting tin and add the short ribs to seal the outside. Remove and set aside.

INGREDIENTS

Serves 4

- Glug of vegetable or sunflower oil
- 4–6 short ribs
- 2 bulbs of garlic
- 2 onions
- 3 carrots
- 300ml red wine
- Petal from a whole star anise

3 Slice the whole garlic bulbs and the onions in half, and place along with the carrots in the bottom of the same tin to form a trivet.

4 Place the ribs on top of this so they're raised up a little and pour over the wine. Add the star anise petal.

5 Place in the oven for 3 hours. The veg will cook down and the meat will go lovely and tender.

6 When done, gently remove the ribs to a warm plate (you can remove the bone if you like – it should just pop out) and put the roasting tin back on the hob on a furious boil to reduce the sauce a little. Squash the garlic into the sauce.

7 Serve with mashed potatoes and plenty of greens.

Meatloaf

A homely dish, much loved in the USA, where traditionally it was made with a mixture of minced beef, pork and veal. Vegetables are added too, to both break up the texture and bulk out the meat – onions obviously, but also garlic, carrots, tomatoes, peppers, spinach, and I've even seen gherkins added. Eggs and breadcrumbs help bind the mixture then it's just a question of baking it. Equally enjoyable hot, smothered in barbecue sauce, or cold on a picnic.

INGREDIENTS

Serves 4–6
- Glug of vegetable or sunflower oil
- 500g minced meat (allow 300g beef to 200g pork or sausage meat)
- 1 large onion, diced
- 1 clove of garlic, crushed
- 1 carrot, grated
- 2 slices of stale or toasted bread, blitzed into crumbs
- Plenty of salt and pepper
- 2 dashes of Worcestershire sauce
- Small bunch of parsley finely chopped
- 1 teaspoon of oregano
- 1 teaspoon of thyme
- 1 egg, beaten

For the glaze
- Barbecue sauce or homemade ketchup

METHOD

1 In a frying pan, soften the onions, garlic and carrot in a little oil and set aside to cool. Top tip: you can blitz the onions, carrot and garlic (as well as any other vegetables you fancy adding) in a food processor after making the breadcrumbs.

2 Place the minced meat in a bowl, add the onions, any vegetables and all the other ingredients and combine well using your hands.

3 Place the meat mixture in a loaf tin or enamel tin. Place this in a larger ovenproof dish and half fill with water.

4 Bake in the oven for 1 hour until the meat shrinks away from the tin. Allow to cool a little so some of the fat and meat juices are reabsorbed. Finally, turn out onto a plate, brush with sauce and slice.

Asian-style beef noodle soup

This is exactly the sort of dish to make on a Monday evening with leftover beef and homemade stock from Sunday's roast. You can customise it as much as you like: either cook the noodles separately in boiling water or cheat and cook them in the stock. The only thing to watch out for is timing; you want any vegetables to be cooked but still crunchy. Larger items like green beans will take longer to cook than spinach.

INGREDIENTS

Serves 2, but up the amounts for more mouths

Base ingredients
- 500ml beef stock
- 1 ball of noodles per person
- Handful of beef strips per person

Sauce extras (a dash or two of any of the following:)
- Teriyaki sauce
- Soy sauce
- Miso paste
- Chilli bean sauce
- Wasabi paste
- Nam pla (fish sauce; go easy with this, it's very pungent)

Dry spices (a pinch or two of any of the following:)
- Chilli flakes
- Cinnamon
- Star anise
- Sesame seeds

Fresh ingredients (to taste)
- A few slices of fresh chilli
- Small bunch of coriander or parsley, roughly chopped
- A squeeze of lime juice
- Soft boiled egg (half per person)
- A few slices of fresh ginger
- Slices of garlic

Vegetables (rough handful of any of the following:)
- Bok choi
- Sliced green beans
- Spinach
- Bean sprouts
- Soya beans (can be from frozen)

METHOD

1 In a large saucepan, heat the beef stock up to boiling and add any additions you're planning on using.
2 Turn down to a simmer. Add the noodles and any vegetables and cook through. Finally, add the slices of roast beef to just warm through.
3 Use tongs to place a selection of all the ingredients in a bowl, and then top with a ladle of the stock. Garnish with fresh chilli and coriander to taste.

CHAPTER 5
LAMB

Around 60% of Britain – particularly Scotland, Wales and the north of England – is cold, wet, hilly and covered in grass. While rubbish for agriculture, these conditions are perfect for sheep production. Such is the versatility of sheep that they can even live on seaweed by the sea, as do those on North Ronaldsay in Scotland or on the salt marshes of Essex. Historically, sheep provided not only wool, but milk too. Meat was the by-product after an animal had become older.

A quick word about goat. Goat meat's production is on the rise in the UK, if only to stop unwanted Billies from being slaughtered at birth (they can't produce goat milk unlike females), so if you do see some, buy it. In many of the slow-cooked recipes, you can swap lamb for goat.

Types of lamb

Sheep production is stratified into three main types, with different breeds living in different environments: namely hill and mountain breeds, upland breeds and lowland breeds. There are thought to be more sheep breeds in the UK than in any other country in the world, with 106 breeds being found in an audit of 2012. Here are just a few:

LLEYN

A medium-sized lowland sheep and the most popular non-hill breed in the UK, weighing up to 70kg, fully grown.

TEXEL

A fast-growing sheep, originally from Holland and introduced to the UK in the 1970s. It produces a lean carcass, has good muscle development and has become the most popular terminal sire breed in the UK.

CHEVIOT

Hardy upland wool and meat breed from the Cheviot Hills between Scotland and England; your classic big woolly hillside sheep.

HERDWICK

LAMB Under 1 year old.

HOGGET Between 1 and 2 years old, has a slightly stronger flavour.

MUTTON Over 2 years old, with a much stronger flavour.

KID Goat meat up to 14 months old, sometimes called the Portuguese word *cabrito*.

HERDWICK
Grey-coloured, very hardy sheep, native to the Lake District. It produces a unique type of wool and strong, flavourful meat. Much beloved by Beatrix Potter.

SUFFOLK
A fast-growing, large sheep, with a black face and legs and a white coat. Suffolk sheep are one of the most popular sheep varieties globally.

THE MANX LOAGHTAN
Pronounced *lock-ton,* this primitive rare breed sheep from the Isle of Man produces stunning rich, dark meat, more akin to venison. They're stunning to look at, with a mousey brown coat that gives them their name and two pairs of horns.

Rare breed animals tend to produce highly flavourful meat, but are often too small to kill as lambs, instead they're grown on as hogget or mutton.

SUFFOLK

THE MANX LOAGHTAN

Main cuts of lamb

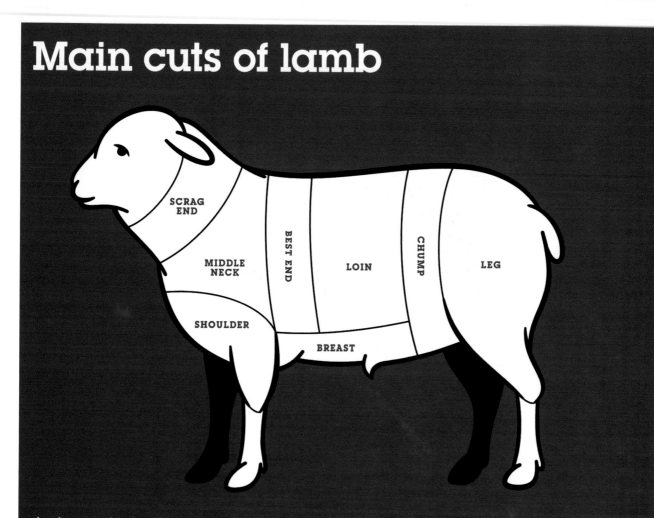

Lambs are cut into four: the forequarter, the middle or saddle, the breast and the leg (at the rear). From there, they're further broken down into specific cuts.

SCRAG END
From the neck of the animal. It has a lot of bones in it, so needs slow cooking to loosen them. They do give a good flavour, however.

MIDDLE NECK
More meat and less bone than scrag, and just as flavourful. Again, best slow-cooked. Meat from here is often minced.

SHOULDER
Not as easy to carve as a leg, but still good. Can be boned and rolled (a big job), and stuffed. Best cooked slower than you would a leg.

BEST END (OF NECK)
Also known as a rack of lamb and made up of the first eight ribs. Can be cooked and served as a rack, or cut into individual cutlets. Removing the eye of the meat entirely gives you lamb noisettes.

BREAST
From the belly area, this contains a lot of fat. Often sold rolled which needs long, slow cooking to render out the fat.

LOIN
The loin gives us a saddle of lamb, which is a great roasting joint. It's from here we also get Barnsley chops.

CHUMP
Where the loin joins the back legs. It can also be roasted, stewed or cut into chump chops, as well as boned and rolled.

LEG
The most popular cut of lamb, which is best roasted and served pink, but can also be slow-cooked. Once boned out, it can also be stuffed. Slices across the leg give steaks. Finally under this, there's the shank.

Roast leg of lamb

Rosemary, garlic, salt – so says Uncle Monty from the classic cult movie *Withnail & I*, and he's not wrong. These three additions make a good leg of lamb great.

For this recipe, I've used a flavour injector to add pureed garlic and white wine directly into the meat. If you've not got one of these just make small slits in the meat and add slivers of whole garlic.

This is a two-stage cooking process. First, I've browned the outside of the meat on the hob to add colour and to keep the juices in, and then it's a long, slow roast in the oven to cook it through.

INGREDIENTS

Serves 4–6
- 1 leg of British lamb (1.5–2kg)
- 2 cubes of frozen garlic or a large squeeze of garlic from a tube
- 1 glass of white wine
- Vegetable oil for frying in
- Sprigs of rosemary
- 2 pinches of sea salt

METHOD

1 Take the lamb out of the fridge 30 minutes before you want to start cooking.
2 First make the garlic puree. In a mini food processor, place the garlic, salt and wine, and blitz to a runny consistency. Alternatively, place it in a mug and blitz it with a stick blender.

Place the roasting tray on the hob, add the oil and heat until smoking hot.
3 Add the lamb to the tin and move around every 3 minutes until the surface is sealed completely. Leave both the lamb and the tin to cool down then wipe out the tin and place a wire rack in it.
4 Heat the oven to 100°C.
5 Break off sprigs of rosemary and have these standing by. Load the flavour injector with the garlic and wine mixture and slowly inject the meaty

parts of the lamb with it. When you remove the needle from the lamb, stuff a spring of rosemary in the hole. Repeat 10 or so times all over the meat.
6 Place the lamb on the rack and in the oven for 3.5 hours. Check after 3 hours with your meat thermometer: you want an internal temperature of 55°C for medium rare. Leave to rest for 20 minutes before carving.

TOP TIP:

With the oven set so low, you'll need to get your roasties in much sooner than normal, at around the 2 hour mark. You can then crank up the heat to 230°C once the lamb is out and resting to give them a final blast.

Slow-cooked shoulder of lamb

Shoulder is cheaper than leg of lamb, and because of the placement of the bones, it isn't as easy to carve. Consequently, slow-cooking it is a much better method of cooking it, enabling it to be shredded apart. Good as it is, it's also a cut that works with rubs – or in this case, flavour injecting. If you've not got a flavour injector (see page 16) you could make the mixture, cut small slashes in the meat and apply the flavour that way.

INGREDIENTS

Serves 4–6

- 1 small glass of white wine
- Cube of frozen garlic, defrosted or two fresh cloves, peeled
- 2 sprigs of rosemary
- 1 lemon, juice and zest
- 3 onions
- Approx. 2kg shoulder of lamb
- 1 tablespoon of honey
- 1 tablespoon of vegetable oil

METHOD

1 Heat the oven to 220ºC.

2 To make the flavouring, place the wine, garlic, rosemary and lemon juice and zest in a mini blender and blitz; alternatively use a stick blender. You want it fairly slack and runny, so it'll go into the injector.

3 Suck up the flavouring into the syringe and inject the meat, ensuring that you put your thumb or finger over the hole when you remove the needle so the marinade doesn't just ooze out.

4 Add the oil to the roasting tray, followed by the onions sliced in half. Place the lamb on top of the onions or use a rack in the tray to support it. Brush the lamb with the honey. Place in the hot oven for 25 minutes to get a little colour on the flesh.

5 Remove the lamb and turn the oven down to 150ºC (leaving the door open to let out excess heat will quicken this process).

6 Cover the lamb with foil and return to the cooler oven for 4 hours. It's done when you can shred it with two forks.

7 Serve with anything you fancy: wraps and salad, summer vegetables, such as ratatouille, or roast potatoes are great.

Lamb shanks braised with cinnamon and tomatoes

Shanks used to be much cheaper, then in the 1990s chefs and food writers cottoned on to how tasty they were and the price shot up, where it's remained ever since. They're best cooked slowly in a liquid: stock, wine, tomato sauce or curry – they're found across multiple cuisines and can be served with everything from mash to pasta to rice.

With the recipe below, I'm on the coast of the Aegean Sea somewhere, with a Greek-style sauce featuring plenty of tomatoes and cinnamon.

INGREDIENTS

Serves 4

- 2–3 tablespoons of vegetable or sunflower oil
- 4 lamb shanks
- 2 onions, diced
- 1 carrot, finely diced
- 1 stick of celery, finely diced
- 2–3 cloves of garlic, crushed
- 1 teaspoon of tomato puree
- 1 stick of cinnamon
- 1 bay leaf
- 1 teaspoon of dried oregano
- 1 can of plum tomatoes, blitzed
- 200ml stock
- 200ml white wine
- Salt and pepper

METHOD

1 Heat the oven to 160°C.
2 Add some vegetable oil to a casserole and place on a medium heat. Brown the shanks one at a time on all sides and set aside. Turn down the heat, add a little more oil and add the onion, carrot and celery.
3 Cook until softened then add the garlic for a few minutes, before adding the tomato puree and cooking for a few more minutes. Blitz the tomatoes with a stick blender.
4 Add the cinnamon, bay leaf, oregano, salt and pepper, followed by the blitzed tomatoes, stock and wine. Bring up to a gentle boil then add the shanks back to the pot.
5 Transfer to the oven and cook with the lid on for about 2 hours. Check and turn the shanks after 1 hour.
6 Serve with pasta or bread to mop up the sauce.

'Park railings'

Breast of lamb has to be one of – if not the – cheapest cut on the animal. It comes from the belly of the beast, but hasn't the glamour of belly pork. It contains a lot of fat, which you must render off. It's one of the few cheap as chips, tough as old boots, can't even give it away cuts, which with the added magic ingredient of slow cooking and lots of time becomes utterly sublime.

This specific recipe has two names, *Lamb Sainte Menehould* in French, and 'park railings' in English. It's essentially a lamb version of fish fingers, but far, far better. Seldom seen on restaurant menus, sadly. Now, it does take a bit of time to make; like many recipes in this book it's not a just-back-from-work midweek supper. It's more a stunning starter for a special feast, but again, do the lamb prep the day before.

. . . .

INGREDIENTS

Serves around 6 as a starter, or 4 as a main

For the breast of lamb

- 2 carrots
- 1 onion
- 1 stick of celery
- 3 cloves of garlic
- 1.5kg lamb breast, unrolled (with bones in if you can get them, don't worry if not)
- A few black peppercorns
- 1 bay leaf
- Small glass of white wine

For the coating

- 2 eggs
- 200g panko breadcrumbs
- 2 tablespoons of flour
- Around 4 tablespoons of English mustard
- 2 litres of vegetable oil for deep fat frying

METHOD

1 Peel and roughly chop the vegetables. Place in a shallow baking dish along with the lamb, peppercorns, bay leaf and wine.

2 Place in the oven at 140ºC for 4 hours until the lamb is completely cooked and any bones can be pulled away with ease, leaving you with just the meat.

3 Next you want to chill and press it. Take a baking tray with a small lip and line with cling film. Carefully lift the lamb breast out of the dish it was cooked in with a couple of fish slices, drain, and place on the cling film-lined baking tray.

4 Fold the cling film over the meat to totally envelop it, place a book (not this one) or small chopping board or a piece of wood on top, and weigh it down with a few tins. Leave to cool down and then place this in the fridge to set firm.

5 The next day, the remaining fat in the lamb should have set it. Take a very sharp knife and slice the cold lamb into fish finger-style pieces.

6 Beat the eggs together on a plate, and have the breadcrumbs and flour on separate plates too. Dust lightly with the flour, then spread one side of each lamb finger with the mustard. Dip into the egg with your left (wet) hand. Transfer to the breadcrumbs and coat the lamb fingers using your (dry) right hand.

7 Heat the vegetable oil in a deep fat fryer or a wok and fry the lamb fingers until golden brown.

8 Best served as a starter with a punchy sauce; blitz mayonnaise, capers, tarragon and salt and pepper. Oddly, tartare sauce works well too, just add chopped capers to mayonnaise.

Lamb chops

Some of the best lamb chops are to be found in Tayyabs restaurant in London's Whitechapel (The Lehore Kebab house is pretty good too) – so much so, it's practically their signature dish. Their recipe is a closely guarded secret, so here's my take on Indian-style lamb chops.

INGREDIENTS

Serves 4–6
- Thumb-sized piece of fresh ginger
- 2 cloves of garlic
- 4 tablespoons of yogurt
- 2 teaspoons of chilli powder
- 1 teaspoon of dried coriander
- 1 teaspoon of ground cumin
- 1 teaspoon of ground cinnamon
- 1 teaspoon of mild curry powder
- 1 teaspoon of mango chutney
- 4–6 lamb chops

To serve
- 1 lemon

METHOD

1 To make the marinade, place the ginger and garlic in a mini blender and blitz or smash with a pestle and mortar until paste-like. Mix into the yoghurt, along with all the other ingredients.

2 Using a rolling pin, bash the chops slightly to flatten them, and then pour the marinade over. Leave for at least 3 hours, though overnight is better. You can even leave them for up to 2 days.

3 When you're ready to cook them, scrape off any excess marinade. Heat the grill to 180°C and grill on both sides, turning occasionally for 10–15 minutes until done. Alternatively, cook on the barbecue.

4 Squeeze a little lemon over just before serving with a raita to cool things down.

Barnsley chop

The Barnsley chop is believed to have originated at Brooklands Hotel (now a Holiday Inn) in Barnsley. Such was the fame of this restaurant in the town that in 1984, *The New York Times* paid a visit and spoke to the then proprietor, who replied 'up here, they expect to see some mass on the dinner table'.

Others, though, claim it was the King's Head Hotel on Market Hill that served it first in 1849. It first appears in print in *Bradshaw's Illustrated Tourists' Handbook* of 1858, and seems to have been a speciality enjoyed by farmers when down from t'hills on market day.

Whoever first served it doesn't really matter, what does matter is size. This is not only a double chop, it's a thick double-chop taken from the first three ribs after the shoulder, right across the carcass, and should be around 3cm thick. Best served with mash or chips.

. . . .

INGREDIENTS
Serves 2
- 2 large Barnsley chops
- Salt, to season
- Knob of butter

. . . .

METHOD
1 Heat a heavy-bottomed pan until smoking. Season the flesh of each chop on both sides. Hold both chops together using a pair of tongs and position so you can place the fat edge on the pan first. Do this and slowly rock it around to render the fat a little and get a little colour on it.
2 When you've done this, place the chops flesh-side-down separately and cook for 8 minutes then flip over for another 3–4 minutes.
3 Turn out the heat, add a knob of butter and baste the chops, before leaving to rest somewhere warm for 3 minutes.

YORKSHIRE SAUCE

Keep things in God's Own County and serve with Yorkshire sauce. Heat a glass of port in a small saucepan and add a very finely diced shallot as well as thyme, redcurrant jelly and the zest of an orange.

French-trimmed rack of lamb

The most expensive cut on the lamb (which is why it also goes by the name 'best end'), so you need to be careful when preparing and cooking it. It's best to start the rack off in a pan to get some colour on the meat, before finishing it in the oven.

FRENCH TRIMMING

Lamb (as well as most other meats) can be French-trimmed. This calls for the removal of the meat at the top of the ribs to expose about 4–5cm of the rib bone. Cut along the outside of the meat just above the eye of the loin. Turn the loin over and cut each 'chunk' of flesh out from between each rib. After each piece comes out, scrape the bones clean. Don't throw the trimmings away – save them for other things, or stock at the very least. Also, wrapping the bones in foil during cooking will keep them pale and stop them getting too dark as they roast.

Can you still buy those little paper hats to put on the ends of the ribs? Probably, but these days they're very much optional. In French they're known as *manchettes* and were originally to allow the carver to hold the meat firmly without getting greasy.

INGREDIENTS

Serves 6–8

- 1 French-trimmed rack of lamb, 6–8 chops (1 per person)
- Salt and pepper, to season
- Vegetable oil

METHOD

1 Heat the oven to 220°C.
2 Score any surface fat present on the rack of lamb in a criss-cross pattern with a sharp knife, or if there's a lot present, remove most of it. Cover the ribs with foil and heat a heavy ovenproof pan, large enough to hold the rack. Alternatively, use the flat side of a griddle. Rub the lamb with a small amount of oil, and season.
3 When the pan is smoking hot, add the lamb, fat-side-down, and cook for around 2 minutes until sealed. Repeat with the ribs side (a little harder to do) and each end for 1 minute apiece.
4 Transfer to the oven, cook for 8–10 minutes and check the internal temperature: rare should be 60°C, medium 65°C and anything over that – well to be honest, you've ruined it.
5 Rest somewhere warm for 10 minutes before serving.

OTHER OPTIONS

STUFFING: You can cut between each rib, halfway into the eye of the meat, and stuff this area with anything from spinach and pine nuts to tomatoes and feta.
CRUST: You can also apply a crust to the flesh side of the meat (don't brown it first, though). Crusts should be made up mainly of breadcrumbs, with a few punchy aromatics in like herbs or spices. Paint English mustard onto the meat with a pastry brush to help adhere the crumb to the flesh. Then roast in a 200°C oven for around 12–15 minutes for medium-rare and leave to rest for 10 minutes.

Koftas

Lamb mice is great value for money and koftas are one of the easiest ways to put it to good use, especially if you've got a crowd coming. This recipe features the classic double act of much of Levant cookery: cumin and cinnamon, to which I've added chilli for heat and mint for flavour. If you've got an old coffee grinder or a mini blender, grind the spices fresh – they'll have much more zing.

You can make long ones on wooden skewers, or little bite-sized ones on cocktail sticks for something a bit more fancy. I love these on flat breads with a range of dips from hummus (available everywhere) to muhammara (not so widely available) – a smoky red pepper and walnut sauce originally from Aleppo in Syria. A salad of shredded lettuce is often present, but seldom takes part in proceedings.

. . . .

INGREDIENTS

Makes around 6–10 koftas, depending on how long and thick you make them

- 800g lamb mince
- 2 teaspoons of ground cinnamon
- 2 teaspoons of ground cumin
- 1 teaspoon of chilli flakes
- 1 tablespoon of finely chopped mint
- Salt and pepper

TOP TIP:
THE DOUBLE SKEWER METHOD

Most recipes instruct you to shape the meat around a stick and start cooking. The trouble with this is that as the meat cooks, it contracts and loses its grip on the stick. You can then find yourself trying to turn the kofta over to cook the other side, and having it spin on the stick, cooked side already down. By forming your meat around TWO sticks side-by-side, the meat can't spin around and you can turn over your koftas in the pan or barbecue easily. Also, pre-soaking the sticks in water can stop them burning if you're cooking over flames. You read it here first.

METHOD

1 Soak your skewers if you need to, and have them arranged in pairs on your board. Have a baking tray or plate ready on which to put the shaped koftas.

2 Using your hands, mix the lamb and spices together in a large bowl. Hold a pair of skewers in your hand and scoop up a piece about the size of a snooker ball with the other one. Gently squash into a sausage shape around the skewers, making sure that the skewers are in the centre of the formed meat and that the surface is even. Place on the tray and repeat until all the mixture is used. A spell in the fridge wouldn't hurt just to firm them up again (you can do all this the day before, too).

3 Cook over a high heat on a griddle or shallow-sided pan, or over the barbecue for about 10 minutes, turning regularly.

Lancashire hot pot

Hot pot means something to the people of Lancashire. It's one of a number of cheap, comforting, homely dishes made with lamb or mutton from all sides of the Irish Sea; think Scouse in Liverpool, Tatie Pot in Cumbria, and Irish Stew.

INGREDIENTS

Serves 4–6

- 1kg 'scrag end' neck of lamb
- 20g plain flour
- 40g butter, plus more for the top
- 2 large onions, finely sliced
- 2 carrots, peeled and cut into chunks
- 1 celery stick, sliced
- Dash of Worcestershire sauce
- Salt and pepper, to season
- 300ml stock
- 800g potatoes, thinly sliced

The late actress Betty Driver MBE, who played Betty Williams for 42 years on *Coronation Street* and became famous for her on-screen hot pot, once said that she couldn't 'actually make one to save her life', as she didn't eat meat!

Traditionally, it was made with mutton and if you can get it, it will make a much more flavourful stew. Try the usual places such as farm shops, online or asking your butcher. The cut you want to use is the lovely sounding 'scrag end' from the neck of the animal. They're basically big, thick boney bits. It's a very cheap, tough cut that needs – you've guessed it – long, slow cooking. Neck fillet is something different and often much more expensive.

There's no point making this with fancy cuts and starting off with olive oil and the like – simplicity and purity is key here. I think this is best made in a traditional stoneware dish with a lid so there's no browning of the meat first; it's just assembled and put in the oven. You can, of course, use a metal casserole.

METHOD

1. Heat the oven to 180ºC.
2. Dust the lamb pieces with the flour and place in the hot pot dish. In a frying pan, melt the butter on a low heat and soften the onion, carrot and celery. Add to the hot pot on top of the lamb. Add a dash of Worcestershire sauce, plenty of salt and pepper and as much stock to cover, saving a teacup's worth for later. You want everything snug together in the dish.
3. Thinly slice the potatoes – a mandolin makes slicing the potatoes easier, if more dangerous; otherwise just use a knife and try to slice about as thick as a pound coin. Top with the slices of potato: start with the small end pieces (these will cook down and thicken the sauce) and end with the larger, best-looking pieces as the final top layer. Pour the remaining stock over the potatoes so it slowly trickles down, and dot each slice with a small knob of butter.
4. Place in the oven for 20 minutes, then turn the heat down to 130ºC and cook for 2 hours. For the final 30 minutes, turn the heat back up to 180ºC and remove the lid until the potatoes are golden brown.
5. This is traditionally served with pickled red cabbage and plenty of bread and butter to soak up the 'jipper'.

Moussaka

In most people's minds, moussaka is a Greek dish, but variations of it are actually found right across what was once the Ottoman Empire, including the Balkans, Turkey and the Levant. Balkan versions substitute potatoes for aubergines, while the Turkish version isn't layered in construction, but served more like a stew.

INGREDIENTS

Serves 4–6

- 2–3 aubergines
- 2–3 tablespoons of vegetable oil
- 500g lamb mince
- 1 onion, finely diced
- 3 cloves of garlic, crushed
- 2 teaspoons of ground cinnamon
- 1 teaspoon of oregano, fresh or dried
- 1 teaspoon of dried mint
- 500g passata
- 100ml red wine

For the béchamel sauce topping

- 50g butter
- 45g flour
- 300ml milk
- 50g grated Parmesan or pecorino cheese
- Pinch of nutmeg
- Salt and pepper, to season
- 1 egg, beaten

METHOD

1 Heat the oven to 180°C.

2 Slice the aubergines lengthways into slices around 1cm thick, add a few glugs of oil to a frying pan and fry each one until golden brown and soft. They'll absorb a lot of the oil, depending on how big they are and how thick you've cut them, so have plenty standing by. (You can also do this stage in the oven if you prefer, just brush the slices with the oil and cook on a baking sheet.) Remove with tongs and set to drain on kitchen paper.

3 To make the meat filling, add a tablespoon of oil to a high-sided frying pan or casserole. On a high heat, brown the minced lamb then add the diced onion and cook until soft.

4 Add the garlic, herbs and spices, followed a few minutes later by the passata and wine. Bring up to a simmer and leave to gently cook for around 30 minutes. You want a dry-ish mixture.

5 To make the béchamel sauce, gently melt the butter in a saucepan. Add the flour and stir the mixture vigorously with a spoon. It will clump together, but keep stirring; you want to cook the flour in the butter. When it's settled down a bit and returned to a more liquid state, add cold milk a little at a time. It will immediately turn solid again, but just keep gently stirring. As the sauce becomes liquid you may want to switch to using a whisk. Add the cheese, nutmeg and the seasoning and turn out the heat. Leave to cool, then add the beaten egg, stirring well.

6 Place half the slices of aubergine in the bottom of an ovenproof dish, then spoon over half of the meat mixture. Cover this with the remaining slices of aubergine and the rest of the meat. Smooth down and then add the béchamel topping.

7 Bake in the oven for around 40 minutes until the topping is a lovely golden brown. Leave to cool and set before serving.

Lamb curry

Curry is one of those ever-forgiving meat dishes that can be tweaked and adjusted in any number of ways. This is my standard version, but sometimes I might add spinach or potatoes instead of the tomato. It's a dish you want to take your time over, however. Don't rush it, especially the onions. Also, always make too much, as you can freeze it or have it for lunch the next day. Ramp up the chilli amounts if you like it hotter.

OPTIONS

- Swap out the lamb for diced beef.
- Reduce the tomato content and add fresh spinach and chickpeas.

INGREDIENTS

Serves 4–6

- 3 tablespoons of vegetable oil
- 4 large onions, finely sliced
- 1kg leg of lamb on the bone, cut into bite-sized pieces
- 1 cube of frozen garlic or two cloves, crushed
- 1 cube of frozen ginger or a thumb-sized piece, crushed
- 5 tomatoes, deseeded and chopped
- 2 teaspoons of ground coriander seeds
- 2 teaspoons of ground cumin
- 2 teaspoons of turmeric
- 1 teaspoon of mild chilli powder
- 1 teaspoon of garam masala
- 2 tablespoons of Greek yoghurt
- Salt and pepper

To serve

- 2 red chillies, finely sliced
- Bunch of coriander, chopped

METHOD

1 Add 2 tablespoons of oil to the pan and add the sliced onions. Cook very slowly over a low heat until soft. Remove the onions and wipe out the pan.

2 Turn up the heat, add another tablespoon or so of oil and add the cubed lamb and the bones, if you have any. Brown the lamb.

3 Turn down the heat and return the onions to the pan. Add the garlic, ginger and tomatoes and cook until soft. Slacken with a little water if needed. Place all the spices in a separate dry frying pan and toast gently for a minute, before adding to the curry. Add the salt and pepper.

4 Finally, add the Greek yoghurt and cook either on a low heat in the oven (150°C) or on the hob for about 40–50 minutes, stirring occasionally until the lamb is tender.

5 When done, turn out the heat and let it rest for 5 minutes before adding the fresh chilli and coriander.

6 Serve with naan bread, rice and pickles.

Curried goat

Goat's very much the new kid on the block (sorry…) compared to other meats, but we're slowly getting our head around the idea of eating goat meat these days. After all, we happily tuck into goats' cheese; why not goat meat?

Indeed, demand for cheese made from goats' milk means many billy goats are euthanised shortly after birth. That's not right; far better to let them grow up and eat them. Thankfully, there are a couple of really good goat farmers doing just that.

You can use it just as you would lamb or mutton, but I think the best way is in this classic curry from the West Indies.

INGREDIENTS

Serves 4–6

- 2 tablespoons of vegetable oil
- 1kg lean goat meat
- 2 onions, chopped
- 2 tablespoons of Caribbean curry powder (or use mild)
- 1 Scotch bonnet chilli, chopped
- 10 allspice berries, crushed
- Thumb-sized piece of root ginger, grated
- 2 spring onions
- 2 large tomatoes, chopped
- 400ml vegetable or light chicken stock
- 1 tablespoon of HP sauce
- 2 cloves of garlic, crushed
- Salt and pepper

CHILLI TIPS

Scotch bonnets come in at 100,000–350,000 Scoville units (the Scoville is the measure of how hot peppers are: an ordinary red pepper is 0 while the Carolina Reaper chilli is 1,569,300!), so they're pretty fiery. Consequently, handle with care, and I wouldn't recommend touching your eyes after chopping them!

METHOD

1 Heat a glug of oil in a casserole. Lightly brown the goat meat in small batches and set aside.

2 Turn down the heat, add a little more oil to the casserole and sweat the onions until soft.

3 Add the curry powder, chilli, allspice berries, grated ginger and spring onions and cook for 5 minutes.

4 Add the tomatoes, stock and HP sauce, then return the goat meat to the pan and stir well.

5 Bring to the boil then turn down the heat and either cook on a low simmer for 3 hours, stirring occasionally, or place in a low oven (150°C). It's ready when the sauce has reduced and the meat is tender.

6 Serve with 'rice and peas' – the 'peas' are actually kidney beans – and some fresh coriander.

CHAPTER 6
GAME

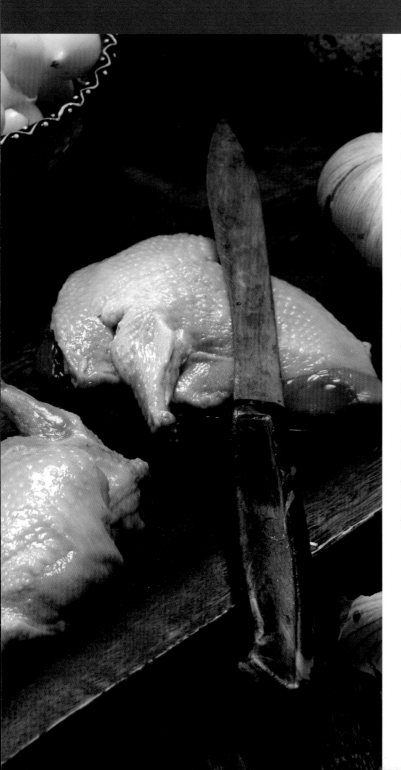

If you ask people if they would like a totally free-range, often organic, low-fat British meat that's plentiful and yet affordable, they'd say 'sure'. Then you mention game and they mumble something and start making their excuses. I've met people who get squeamish about pheasant, but will happily scoff a box of battery-farmed mystery chicken from somewhere in the Far East.

And yet game is all of those things. We should really be eating more of it, especially in the cooler months. Part of what puts people off is the old wives' tale that game must be 'high'; this isn't the case any more. Tastes have changed, softened actually, and we like our game a little less pungent these days. If you think about it, apart from domesticated animals kept mainly for their wool, eggs or milk, all meat was game – be it the deer hunted by the lord of the manor or the rabbit caught by his tenant. Finally, it is apparently illegal to shoot game on a Sunday.

Main types of game

Game comes in two types of packaging: fur and feathers.

VENISON

Lean, fat-free and with a rich, meaty taste. Treat it the same way as beef, but don't overcook it. There are six types of deer in the UK, with most venison coming from red deer.

Season: This depends on location (it's earlier in Scotland) and the sex of the animal (hinds have a shorter season than stags).

WILD RABBIT

Best casseroled or braised slowly, rabbit is very low in fat. Younger ones make the best eating.

Season: All year round.

HARE

Much more than a 'big rabbit', hare has a stronger, more flavourful taste. It doesn't live in burrows, you may be surprised to know. One hare will feed about five people.

Season: 1st January–31st December (England & Wales)
1st October–31st January (Scotland)
12th August–31st January (Northern Ireland).

SQUIRREL

Grey squirrel is available from specialist game dealers. Again, it's very lean, so best casseroled. Red ones are endangered.

Season: All year round.

GROUSE

This has the honour of being the first bird one can shoot of the season, hence the phrase the glorious 12th. It also has the shortest season. Don't eat on the 12th, however, wait until a week or so has passed and they've hung a bit to develop the flavour. Grouse are found on moorland and unique to the British Isles. Best roasted, and a little pink.

Season: 12th August–10th December.

PHEASANT

Everywhere in the countryside in the autumn months, so much so you can 'hunt' them with a car. Pheasant is the most plentiful of our game birds and also the most well-known. Many chicken recipes work with pheasant, but like all game, it is a lot leaner so don't dry it out.

Season: 1st October–1st February.

WOOD PIGEON

Not really considered a true game bird, these are more plentiful than pheasants and even cheaper, as farmers consider them a pest. Their breasts are particularly good pan-fried.

Season: All year round.

PARTRIDGE

Smaller than a pheasant, these are best prepared simply by roasting with a good fatty rasher of bacon across their breasts. There are actually two types in the UK: the grey-legged and the red-legged.

Season: 1st September–1st February.

DUCK AND GOOSE

Wild duck are a totally different texture and flavour to that of farmed versions. Look for wild ones in your butchers during the season.

Season: 1st September–31st January (Inland)
1st September–20th February (Below High Water Mark).

There are many other species of game bird that are shot and are edible, such as ptarmigan, snipe, teal and golden plover, but they're often hard to come by. If you do, simple roasting is often the best treatment. Finally, wild boar are sometimes shot to keep numbers down; if you can get hold of some of that you're very lucky.

Proper paella

Paella is one of those dishes that we're only just learning to pronounce properly, let alone cook properly (it's *pie-ey-ya*, not *pie-ella*, by the way). It comes from Valencia in Spain and was originally a communal meal for those working in the fields. They would put in it whatever they had to hand: snails, rabbit, seasonal vegetables and sometimes chicken.

When the Spanish tourist trade developed in the late 1960s the dish headed to the coast and got a seaside makeover, and it's this version featuring seafood that has become the more well-known version.

PASS THE PAELLA PAN

If it's just the two of you, you can make passable paella in a frying pan. Any more than that, though, and it's worth buying a proper paella pan to do the job. They're available at kitchenware shops, and also online. I've got one I carried all the way back from Spain, as well as a huge gong-like one that I got online, which can feed over ten.

When you get it home you'll need to season it with oil, and never let it sit in water: it'll rust. Non-stick versions are available too.

PAELLA TIPS

- **Don't overload the pan with rice: remember it will swell up when cooked. A rule of thumb is that the rice should never come higher than the handle rivets on each side of the pan.**

- **Don't stir the rice once it's in the pan. Keep the heat low and make sure it doesn't dry out. Eventually a crust (called *socarrat*) will form on the bottom of the pan; this is much desired.**

- **This dish is about using good rice and, secondly, a good stock (though water is traditional): the meat and vegetables shouldn't detract from that. Keep your stockpan hot, and top up with a little hot water if needed.**

- **Obviously you're meant to cook this over a fire stoked by olive branches, all under the shade of a tree – all of which are in a little short supply in Blighty! If you're using a really big pan put it on all four burners, but keep the heat very low and move the pan around to ensure the heat is evenly distributed.**

INGREDIENTS

Serves 6–8

- 2.5 litres of boiling hot chicken stock
- 2 tomatoes, blanched, peeled and diced
- 1 large onion, peeled and finely diced
- Large pinch of saffron
- 200ml olive oil
- 6 chicken thighs, bone removed
- 500g diced rabbit meat and pieces
- 2 cloves of garlic, crushed
- 500g paella rice
- 1 teaspoon of sweet paprika
- Handful of green beans or runner beans, top and tailed (you can pre-cook these first, in which case add them at the end)
- Glass of white wine (an optional luxury not found in the original)
- Handful of chopped parsley

METHOD

1 First, get all the ingredients assembled and ready, and get the stock hot.

2 Make a small cross in the bottom of each tomato. Plunge them into the hot stock for 30 seconds and then remove and wash under a cold tap. You should now be able to peel the skin off easily. Remove the seeds, dice the flesh and set aside with the onion.

3 Put the saffron in a cup with a tablespoon of warm stock to infuse.

4 Add 150ml of oil to the pan. Over a low heat, fry the rabbit pieces and chicken thighs until golden brown.

5 Add the onion, garlic and tomato and gently cook until soft.

6 Add the paprika and the infused saffron, followed by the rice. You might need to add a dash more oil.

7 Warm the rice for a moment and spread it out around the pan then add as much stock to cover it, followed by the green beans. Cook for 10–15 minutes until the rice is tender, but still firm; you might need to add more stock or hot water from the kettle. Don't move it around like you would a risotto.

8 Dig down a little and see if the crust is forming at the bottom. If so, it's done. Turn out the heat, cover with a clean tea towel or foil and allow to rest. The build-up of steam will finish cooking the rice.

Braised rabbit in cider

I had a version of this dish at the River Cottage Canteen – it's a stunner. You'll need to let the rabbit cook slowly in the cider and keep the heat low; otherwise it can turn tough.

RABBIT TIPS

- Wild rabbits are smaller than farmed, but they've had happier lives and taste much, much better. Many farmed rabbits are as intensively reared as bad chicken. Ask your butcher where the rabbit is from before buying.
- The saddles cook faster than the legs; you can add them 30 minutes later if you like.

INGREDIENTS

Serves 4

- 4 rashers of smoked, streaky bacon
- 1 large onion, finely sliced
- 200g whole chorizo or other spicy cured sausage, cut into big chunks
- 6 garlic cloves, peeled
- 2 rabbits, jointed or whole
- 300ml chicken stock
- 1 bottle of good cider
- Small bunch of thyme
- Few grinds of black pepper

METHOD

1. Heat the oven to 150°C.
2. Place a casserole or deep roasting tin that will snuggly hold the rabbits on the hob. Add bacon, onion, chorizo and garlic, and colour a little. Add the rabbits or rabbit pieces and colour a little for about 5 minutes.
3. Add the stock, cider and thyme then season with black pepper.
4. Place in the oven and cook for 2 hours until the rabbit is tender; you want it slightly falling off the bone.
5. When the rabbit is cooked, remove all the pieces, the bacon and the chorizo. Set on a warm plate and cover with a piece of foil and a tea towel.
6. Place the tin or dish back on the hob and give the sauce a good blast of heat to reduce it slightly, and mush down the garlic cloves. Spoon some over the meat, and serve with mash or roasted new potatoes and greens.

Maltese rabbit stew

This is the national dish of Malta, where it's known as *Stuffat tal-Fenek*. It is eaten in two parts. First, some of the sauce is removed and used on pasta as a starter then the rabbit is served with potatoes as a main course. It's a real fill-you-up celebration dish that is often left all day to cook, hence the long cooking time.

Lots of garlic and bay leaves are the two defining flavourings of this dish.

INGREDIENTS
Serves 4–6
- 1 rabbit, joined
- 4 tablespoons of vegetable or sunflower oil
- 300ml red wine
- 5 or 6 cloves of garlic, peeled and lightly crushed
- 2 onions, finely diced
- 1 teaspoon of curry powder
- 5 bay leaves
- 1 litre tomato passata
- 1 tin of peas (optional) or a handful of frozen peas

METHOD
1. Marinade the rabbit in the wine and garlic overnight, then remove and pat dry. Save the marinade and fish out the garlic cloves.
2. Crush the marinated garlic cloves and fry with the onion in oil until soft, then remove and set aside.
3. Re-oil the pan and fry the rabbit in pieces until a golden brown colour.
4. Return the onions to the pan and add the curry powder. Then add the tomato passata and a splash or two of the wine marinade until the rabbit is covered.
5. Cook on a low heat (150°C) for 3 hours, or even overnight at 100°C.
6. About 20 minutes before serving, add the peas.
7. Using a ladle, spoon off some of the sauce and serve over a small bowl of spaghetti as a starter. Then in the same bowl, serve the stew with potatoes roasted with fennel seeds, crusty bread and a bottle of red wine.

Hare ragu with pappardelle

You don't often see hare these days, as there's just not the demand for them there once was. In some areas, however, hunting them is not allowed, while in other parts of the country they're so abundant that some form of control must take place to protect crops, as three full-grown hares can eat as much as a sheep.

INGREDIENTS
Serves 6–10
- 3 onions, finely diced
- 2 sticks of celery, finely diced
- 3 carrots, finely diced
- 1 tablespoon of lard
- 1 hare, jointed (and keep the blood)
- 4 tablespoons of plain flour
- 4 cloves of garlic, crushed
- 3 tins of plum tomatoes, blitzed up
- 1 carton of passata
- 200ml beef stock
- Half a bottle of red wine
- 1 tablespoon of thyme leaves
- Lots of salt and pepper

To serve
- Dash of extra virgin olive oil per person
- 100–150g pappardelle per person
- Grated parmesan cheese

Hare has a strong, gamey flavour and its rich, dark meat is more like venison than rabbit in my mind. A hare will easily feed 6–10 people. Like much game, it's best braised in a liquid slowly, very slowly. This recipe is a Tuscan classic, and sees the hare slow-cooked in tomatoes, wine and stock.

This recipe takes a fair amount of time, if not effort, to do. I cooked this once all day, from 10am to 10pm and then had it the next day. You could of course cook it overnight. Be warned, this recipe makes a lot of ragu. You can either joint the hare and use fewer pieces and half the ingredients, or make it as is and freeze the results in portions.

TIPS
There will be blood. But come on, this is *The Meat Manual*. Yes, you could make a ragu with bog standard supermarket mince, but it won't have any of the flavour. It is because hare is such a strongly flavoured meat, that a little of it goes a very long way. If you can't get hare, but still want something different, try wild boar.

PREPARING YOUR HARE
I'd be tempted to remove the ribcage entirely and not bother cooking it; there's not much meat on it and you'll spend aged picking out the little bones. The same could be said for the spine; do remove the loins from it though, they're very meaty. Your hare might also have its liver still attached – you can finely dice this and add it to the ragu. I wouldn't bother too much with any other offal present however.

METHOD

1 First prepare the vegetables by finely dicing them.
2 Next get your biggest stockpot and melt the lard in it.
3 Dust the hare pieces with a little plain flour, fry quickly to gain a little colour and then set aside.

4 Once done, wipe out the pan, add more fat or oil, and then add the vegetables including the garlic. Stir until softened a little.
5 Put the hare pieces back in and add everything else. Bring up to a simmer then place a cartouche on top and put in a 140°C oven for 8–10 hours, checking occasionally.
6 When the meat is falling off the bone, remove from the oven and tip into a high-sided roasting tray. Leave to cool a little then pick over the ragu, removing any bones that you come across. Place this roasting tin in the oven for a final hour just to reduce the sauce a little more. Check the seasoning at this stage, and you might want to add some shine by drizzling over a little olive oil.
7 Cook the pappardelle, as per the packet's instructions, then combine a little of the sauce with the pasta and grate over fresh Parmesan cheese.

CHAPTER 7
OFFAL

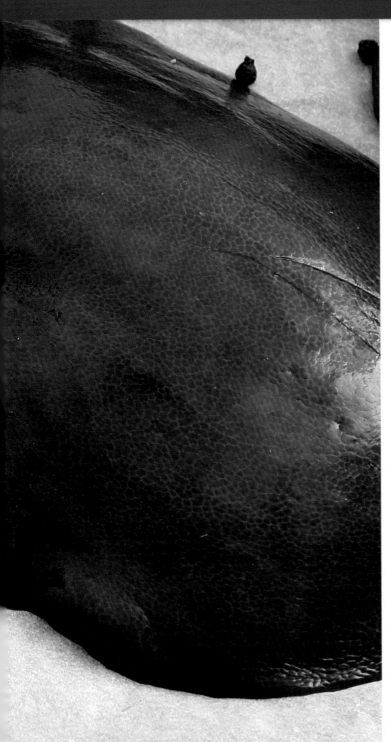

Today, we eat about 70% of the edible meat from a pig. In the past, it was more like 99.9%: every scrap had a purpose and use. If you're squeamish about offal, you need to get a grip; there's plenty of flavour in what's often called the 'fifth quarter'. Yet it's often the bit we throw away, which is a shame, as offal is full of vitamins and often low in fat.

Types of offal include liver, kidneys, heart, sweetbreads, head, gizzards, bones, feet and intestines. In fact, if you've eaten a good quality sausage, you've already eaten intestines, as that's what sausages are made from. There you go, wasn't that bad was it?

Even 20 years ago, people in Britain frequently ate more offal; tripe was much eaten in the north of England. Today, you occasionally see it on restaurant menus, sometimes billed as Apart from liver, which you should always serve pink, offal is often thoroughly cooked. It has great versatility in the kitchen, and can be paired with other meats (think steak and kidney), or incorporated into terrines and pâtés. It's also good on its own, in small amounts and as a starter.

Finally, if you're feeling 'offaly' adventurous, seek out a copy of *Testicles: Balls in Cooking and Culture*, a French book that was translated and reprinted in 2011. It's eye-watering in both its recipes and level of detail, and shows that people in the past were much less squeamish, or perhaps just hungrier, than we are today.

Steak and kidney pudding

This is one of England's greatest dishes, yet it's actually not that old. Mrs Beeton gives us the first written recipe, which she says came to her from a lady in Sussex, a county that was once famous for its puddings.

INGREDIENTS

Serves 4

For the filling

- 1 tablespoon of vegetable oil
- 800g braising steak
- 400g trimmed and prepared kidney
- 4 tablespoons of flour, for dusting the meat
- 1 large onion
- The leaves off 2 sprigs of thyme
- A few sprigs of thyme
- Small handful of dried mushrooms, soaked in warm water (optional)
- A few slugs of Worcestershire sauce
- 400ml beef stock
- 400ml flavourful beer
- A few big grinds of pepper
- A pinch of salt
- A few knobs of butter for buttering your dish

For the pastry

- 400g self-raising flour
- Pinch of salt
- 200g beef suet
- Around 150ml water (enough to bring it together as a dough)

Essentially, you make a stew filling first, and then once cooled, encase it in a pastry crust. However, the crust is made with suet and because the pudding is steamed rather than cooked in an oven, the result is a softer, sponge-like crust.

The choice of kidney is important too. A bad kidney will taste of pee – I'm not really selling this to you, am I?! Try and get really fresh kidneys, as like all offal they deteriorate rapidly. While cows' kidneys might seem the first choice, they can have a very strong taste. Veal kidneys will be less harsh, and lambs' more delicate still.

My advice is start with lamb and work your way up to ox. Please don't leave out the kidneys though;

you'll need that slight earthy offal tang that they give. Whichever kidney you use, you'll need to remove the white central hard core of each one as well as any membrane. Cut the kidney in half and remove the core with a sharp knife.

There are two ways to make this; one sees the raw filling added to the bowl, and the other way calls for the filling to be made first then left to cool before being added. Personally I favour the latter. It means a two-stage process, but will give you a much more consistent result. You can also cook more filling than you need and freeze it.

This will be enough for a 1.5 litre/2pint pudding bowl. You want to make the filling the day before if possible.

METHOD

1 Add the oil to a casserole pan and put on a high heat.

2 Flour the meat in small batches and brown in the pan then set aside.

3 Add the onion and herbs to the pan and soften.

4 Return the meat to the pan and add the stock, beer, Worcestershire sauce and salt and pepper. Also, add the mushrooms, if using, at this stage. Place in a low oven (120°C) and cook for 3 hours. When cooked, leave to cool.

For the pastry

5 Sieve the self-raising flour and salt into a bowl. Add the suet and combine thoroughly.

6 Make a well in the centre and add small amounts of water, slowly bringing the dough together with a spoon until you can get your hands in. It's ready when it's not too wet and no flour remains in the bowl. You might need to add a little extra water.

7 Chill for 15 minutes before using. A rule of thumb for suet pastry is to use around half the weight of suet to flour.

To assemble

8 Butter your pudding dish. Cut off about a quarter of the pastry and set to one side – this will form your lid.

9 Roll out the remaining pastry on a floured surface into a circle shape, about 20cm wide and 1cm thick.

10 Carefully line the pudding dish with the disc of pastry, making sure it's flush with the dish. You want it to come about 1cm over the lip. Roll out the remaining quarter to form your lid.

11 Add your cooled filling mix, then trim off the 1cm lip, brush with water and pop the lid on. You can them trim the excess off and press gently down to get a good seal.

Cooking

12 Put the pudding in a large pan with a lid big enough to hold it and fill with water until it comes halfway up the side of the basin. Put the lid on the pan and simmer for about 3 hours. You might need to top the water up mid-way through.

13 After 3 hours, remove (careful, it'll be hot) and leave to stand for 5 minutes before taking off the pudding basin lid. Turn out onto a warm plate and take to the table with a loud 'ta-da'! Break it gently with a spoon and portion out one of the best dishes you can ever make.

WHAT IS SUET?

Suet is the fat found around the internal organs of animals: mainly pork or beef in the UK. The best suet is found round the kidneys; it's a hard, white, crumbly fat with a pleasant flavour and higher melting point than butter. It comes ready-grated in packets, which makes it much easier to use (must have been a nightmare using it in Victorian times), though some butchers will sell it fresh.

Vegetarian suet is made from palm oil combined with rice flour to resemble real suet; it doesn't have anything like the flavour though. This makes it a better choice for sweet puddings, however.

Liver and sherry

A cheap, traditional British classic, best served with mashed potatoes, onion gravy and peas. It's actually quite a technical dish to pull off: cook the liver too much and it's like leather, too little and there's blood all over your mash, which doesn't look nice.

Like most offal, liver is fairly cheap and really flavoursome. Calves' liver is the most sought-after and relatively the most expensive, after that comes lambs' liver. Ox and pig liver have a stronger taste, with the latter being mainly used in terrines and pâtés.

Do make sure your liver is from animals that have had a free-range or even an organic life. Remember, the liver's job is to filter out toxins and one's belonging to poorly raised animals aren't going to be as good. Unlike other cuts of meat, offal spoils quickly, so it must be either spanking fresh or frozen as soon as it's processed.

INGREDIENTS

Serves 2–3 as a main

- 1 tablespoon of butter
- 1 large onion, finely sliced
- Pinch of salt
- Pinch of sugar
- 500g calves' liver, thinly cut into individual portions
- Flour for dusting
- Glass of sherry (a dark one, such as Amontillado)

METHOD

1 Add half the butter to a frying pan and melt. Add the finely sliced onion, a pinch of salt and a pinch of sugar and cook gently over a low heat for 15 minutes until the onions have really softened and caramelised – this will take longer than you'd think. Meanwhile put some seasoned flour on a plate, dust the liver in it and brush off any excess flour.

2 When the onions are done, remove and set aside. Wipe out the pan with kitchen paper. Add the rest of the butter and turn up the heat until the butter foams.

3 Add the liver to the pan and cook very fast for 2–3 minutes then flip over and cook the other side. For the last 30 seconds throw in the sherry and shake the pan so it ignites (careful here) and burns off the alcohol.

4 Remove the liver onto a clean plate lined with kitchen paper and add the onions back into the pan with the sherry. Stir round completely to make a sauce of sorts. It doesn't need much more to be honest, maybe some bread and a green salad, or perhaps some slow-cooked lentils in winter.

Devilled kidneys

A breakfast dish enjoyed by Edwardian gentlemen in their clubs, as they mused on the passing of Empire. The 'devilling' refers to the strong, piquant sauce in the dish, which you can use to devil other meats.

INGREDIENTS

Serves 2

- 6 lambs' kidneys
- 50g butter
- 2 shallots, peeled and finely chopped
- 1 clove of garlic, peeled and crushed
- 1 teaspoon of cayenne pepper
- 1 teaspoon of English mustard
- 1 teaspoon of Worcestershire sauce
- Splash of double cream
- Salt and pepper
- 2 slices of toast
- Sprinkle of chopped parsley

METHOD

1 First, prepare the kidneys. Cut them in half from top to bottom. Use a small pair of scissors to snip out the white central core and discard.

2 Put a frying pan over a medium heat and melt the butter. Add the kidneys cut-side-down and don't move them for a few minutes, so they get a little colour.

3 Flip the kidneys over, add the shallots and garlic, and cook together.

4 Add the cayenne pepper, English mustard, Worcestershire sauce, salt and pepper and double cream, and cook until the sauce has thickened slightly.

5 Serve hot on a slice of toast. A sprinkle of chopped parsley is all you need as a garnish.

Roast marrow bones

Chef Fergus Henderson has served roasted marrowbone at his St. John restaurant in London since it opened in 1994. As he himself once told me, 'it's a bit cheeky, just roasting bones as a signature dish'. Well, I hope he doesn't mind me cheekily paying homage to it in this book! The dish is startling in its simplicity; consisting of just veal bones, bread, salt, parsley, shallots and capers.

He is by no means the first to cook such a dish, however. Bone marrow on toast was once a favourite dish of Queen Victoria, and her chef Charles Elme Francatelli (an Englishman of Italian extraction) would cook it for her daily. He gives the recipe for *Marrow Toast a la Victoria* in his book *The Cook's Guide, and Housekeeper's &*

Butler's Assistant (1857), which starts with the amusing line, 'procure a marrow-bone, or get the butcher to break the bone for you—as this is rather an awkward affair for ladies'. The bone is poached then served with 'a little chopped parsley, pepper and salt, lemon-juice, and a mere suspicion of shallot'. Note the similarity? You don't

need much with this, just a good piece of sourdough to take the wibberly-wobbly meat marrow, a bit of fresh, acidic punch from the salad and a pinch of salt. It really is one of the best eating experiences there is.

COOKING MARROW

There's a knack to cooking marrow: too little and it'll be raw, too much and it'll render out completely and you'll have 12 hollow bones in a pool of beefy goodness. You want it just quivering and loose from the bone, but not yet melted. Roast for 20 minutes, but check after 15. Allow three pieces of marrow per person.

INGREDIENTS
Serves 4
- 12 pieces of veal bone, between 4–6cm high
- Small bunch of parsley, chopped
- 2 shallots, finely sliced
- 1 tablespoon of drained capers
- A few tablespoons of olive oil and juice of a lemon, mixed together
- Salt and pepper
- 1–2 slices of sourdough bread per person, depending on the size

METHOD
1 Heat the oven to 200ºC.
2 Place the bones in a metal ovenproof dish and bake for 20 minutes, checking after 15.
3 Make the salad by combining the parsley, shallots and capers. Dress with a little olive oil and lemon juice then season well.
4 In a hot griddle pan, toast the sour dough. Plate up at once and serve with a small bowl of sea salt on the table.

Grilled ox heart, salsa and fava bean puree

Ox heart has all the beef flavour for a fraction of the price, coming in at around two quid to a fiver, for even organic ones. However, on the board, it's strikingly anatomical, so be prepared for the fact that, you're basically looking at a cow's huge heart.

Some places sell it ready-trimmed, but if it's not, trim off as much of the exterior fat as you can and remove any silver skin membrane or tubes on the inside. What you're left with is pieces of lean, dark red meat. I always think it's best to treat beef heart like you'd treat squid: cook it for around 30 seconds on a searing hot heat source or for over an hour in a liquid; anything in-between and you'll be eating rubber.

It's a meat that's best used when you want a beefy starter, served with onions and tomatoes in summer, or pureed pulses in cooler months – and that's what I've gone for here. I first had this dish at Trullo restaurant in Islington. Here's my take on it:

INGREDIENTS

Serves 2–4, depending on how much meat you want

- 50ml beef stock
- 1 can of cannelloni beans
- Splash of milk
- Grated Parmesan cheese, to taste
- Salt and white pepper, to season
- 1 ox heart, trimmed and at room temperature
- 1 tablespoon of salsa rossa (optional), or chilli oil and a pinch of chilli flakes

Salsa rossa ingredients
- 2 red peppers
- 2 medium chillies
- 2 tomatoes
- 1 pinch of chilli flakes
- Splash of red wine vinegar

METHOD

1 To make the salsa rossa, remove the stem from two red peppers and two medium-sized chillies. Halve two tomatoes and roast everything in a 200°C oven for 30 minutes.

2 Remove and allow to cool a little, before roughly blitzing in a food processor with a little olive oil, a pinch of chilli flakes and a splash of red wine vinegar. Store in a jam jar: it'll keep for a week in the fridge and is great on everything from a cheese sandwich to pasta.

3 Heat the stock in a small saucepan and add the drained beans. Cook for 15 minutes until the beans have softened a bit, then season well with salt and white pepper and blitz to a puree. You can slacken it with a little milk or cream if it's too thick. You could also add a little Parmesan to up the flavour.

4 Rub a little vegetable oil on the pieces of heart and then heat a griddle pan until they're smoking.

5 Place each piece on the griddle pan and cook for 1 minute each side. Let them rest on a plate. Spoon a small amount of the bean puree onto a plate, and spread out. Place the pieces of beef heart on and drizzle over the salsa rossa or chilli oil.

Chicken liver pâté

A homemade pâté is a great starter. Chicken livers represent excellent value, with a pack of free-range organic ones only costing a few pounds. Once you've got the basic recipe (more of a technique, really) you can start tweaking the flavourings and ingredients: garlic, shallot, mace and nutmeg would all work.

INGREDIENTS

Serves 4–6 as a starter

- 400g free-range chicken livers
- 200g butter, at room temperature
- 3 tablespoons of brandy or Madeira
- A pinch of thyme leaves
- A pinch of salt
- 50ml double cream

METHOD

1 Pat the livers dry on kitchen paper.

2 Place a large knob of the butter in a pan on a high heat and heat until melted. Add the livers and let them colour on the outside, but don't overcook; you want them pink in the middle. Add the brandy, thyme leaves and salt halfway through.

3 Remove and place in a food processor. Blitz and add the cream and the remaining butter gradually.

4 Pass the mixture through a sieve, transfer to individual ramekins or a large dish and smooth down with the back of a spoon.

5 Melt a little extra butter and pour over the top, before placing in the fridge to set.

6 Serve with hot toast and gherkins.

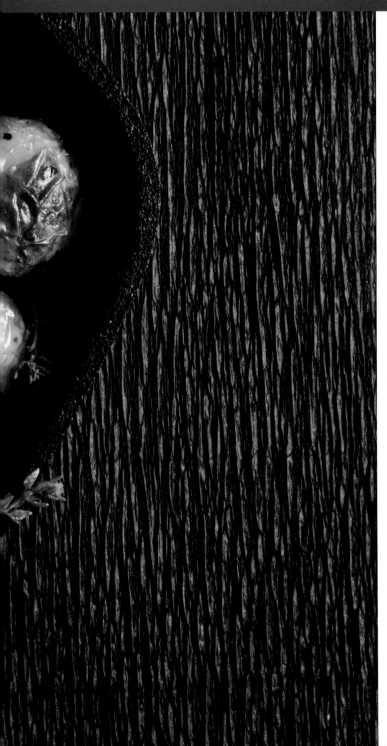

CHAPTER 8
SIDES AND ACCOMPANIMENTS

Where would meat be without its traditional accompaniments? Roast potatoes for Sunday lunch, chips with a steak, creamy mash with a pie. Potatoes in one form or another are the main accompaniment to most meat, along with vegetables, beans or salad. Then there are sauces, dips, marinades and gravy – don't forget the gravy.

There's little point in cooking a great piece of meat, and then sending out pre-bought roasties and instant gravy with it. The accompaniments are just as important as the main event, so here's how to do them right.

Chips

Remember the chip pan? Ours was filled with beef dripping, and as a child I used to love watching it slowly melt to reveal the wire basket within. Of course, they're a total death trap. According to the fire service 'nearly 20 people are killed or injured every day in accidental fires that start in their kitchen, the most common of these caused by deep fat frying'. You don't mess about with a chip pan, chaps.

And so, the oven chip was invented. And yes, they're ok if you're knocking out something quick and easy for the kids, but they're not real chips. Making good chips from scratch and cooking them in fat, or even oil, isn't for the faint-hearted, but well worth it. A small thermostatic (as in you can set the temperature) deep fat fryer costs less that £20 and you can use it for making all sorts of other lovely things like Scotch eggs (page 70) and arancini. If you do opt for the saucepan and basket, get your trusty meat thermometer out, as you'll need to accurately know how hot the fat is. Also, do not overfill your pan with oil; it should be no more than half full according to the fire brigade.

BUT FIRST, A BIT OF RECENT CHIP HISTORY...
In 1993, Heston Blumenthal set about to develop the perfect chip cooking technique. The enemy of chips is moisture inside them (potatoes are mainly composed of water). Heston tried a number of ways to try and remove it, including pricking each chip with a pin to let out the steam. His endeavours resulted in 'triple cooked chips', which first appeared on the menu of The Fat Duck in 1995, and now appear on the menu of pretty much every gastropub and restaurant in Britain.

The traditional way to cook chips – and I know this from a summer job in a Lyme Regis fish and chip shop – was first to blanch or part-cook, but not colour the chips in cooler fat, then cook a second time at a high temperature to colour and crisp them up. Heston took this one stage further, by first part-cooking the chips, not in fat, but in water. The other crucial development was the chilling in the freezer of the chips between each cooking stage.

SIZE MATTERS
You want thin, shatteringly crisp-on-the-outside, fluffy-in-the-middle chips with a steak, not the standard fat, soggy British seaside chip, so cut your potatoes up small. If you've got a mandolin – another terrifyingly deadly piece of kitchen equipment that can easily remove a thumb tip – use that. It'll save time and ensure your chips are of an even size.

Now, I know what you're thinking; exploding chip pans of hot fat, deadly mandolin blades, blast chilling – what a faff over a chip. But don't reach for the oven chips just yet, you can do all the preparation in stages so it's manageable. In effect, it's no more complicated than making roast potatoes.

How to make chips

Maris Pipers or King Edwards are the best potatoes for making chips.

....

INGREDIENTS

Serves 4
- 4 large Maris Piper potatoes
- 2 litres of vegetable oil or 2kg beef dripping (you won't need all of it)
- Salt

....

METHOD

1 Peel and slice the potatoes. You're looking for a height and depth of around 1cm, while the length can be as long as the potato they've come from.

2 Place in a large pan of water and bring to the boil. When they look like they're softening up, use a slotted spoon to remove onto a chopping board lined with kitchen paper, or even better a cake rack, and let them dry off.

3 When cool place in the fridge, or if you've room, the freezer to chill.

4 Heat your oil or fat to 130ºC and cook the chips for around 5 minutes, but don't let them colour.

5 Remove from the fat, turn out the heat and again, let them cool down.

6 Finally, when you're ready to serve, heat the oil up to 180ºC and fry them again to a lovely golden brown.

7 Drain and allow a moment to rest. somewhere warm then sprinkle with sea salt and serve.

Proper mashed potato

There's something about the soft, fluffy buttery-ness of mash that's just perfect with meat like sausages, or a rich, dark stew. Here's how to make utterly perfect mash time after time with pretty much any spud. The secret is... buy a potato ricer.

These handy contraptions squeeze the cooked potatoes through tiny holes into little strands that fall into the waiting bowl. They make making mash a doddle, far easier than all that pounding with a potato masher that the Smash robots found so amusing in the 1970s.

Remember mash isn't just a side, it's 'part of' dishes like cottage pie (page 104). But while the mash for those dishes goes back in the oven allowing any lumpy bits to cook out, mash served straight up is afforded no such luxury. As such, it's got to be top notch.

THE BEST SPUDS

Maris Piper are the universally acknowledged spuds, and they're good, but a bit... well, pedestrian. By all means use them, but keep an eye out for other floury dry varieties out there that will work just as well, if not better. Try to find Mozart, Vivaldi, Rooster, Saxon and hot young newcomer on the culinary potato scene, Vales Sovereign.

LEFTOVERS

You should always make too much mash. Leftovers can be mixed with any vegetables and used in bubble and squeak (page 166). Or if you want to get fancy you could make Duchess potatoes: spoon the cold mash into a piping bag and pipe it into little cones, before transferring to a hot oven to brown.

How to make mash

INGREDIENTS

Serves 4 (with some left over)

- 6 large potatoes
- 20g butter, at room temperature
- Splash of milk
- Pinch of salt

METHOD

1. Peel and quarter the potatoes. Allow one large potato or two small ones per person.
2. Place in a large pan of cold water and bring to the boil
3. Turn down to a gentle rolling boil. You don't want to fast boil potatoes, like you might pasta.
4. After about 15–20 minutes poke a skewer or small knife into the centre of the largest spud. If it gives easily, they're probably done.
5. Remove and drain, then leave in the colander for 10 minutes. This step is very important – right now those potatoes are soaking wet, and they need time to dry out. Mashing them now will give you watery mash. Instead wait until you can see little white dry bits on the edges.
6. Place each quarter into your potato ricer and squeeze into the pan. Add a huge knob of butter, a dash of milk or cream, and gently mix together.

ADDITIONS TO MASHED POTATO

Garlic is a great addition to mashed potatoes. Peel 4 or 5 cloves and infuse in melted butter on the lowest heat your hob will do.

There's a French dish called aligot that sees garlic, milk and cheese added to mashed potatoes that are then beaten until they almost become as stretchy as a fondue.

MORE BUTTER

The French chef Joel Robuchon is famous for using half as much butter as potato in his recipe. He also cooks his potatoes in their skins, then peels once they're cool enough to handle.

CHEESE

Cheesy mash is ace, isn't it? You'll need something with a strongish flavour – a good cheddar, or one of the nuttier northern European cheeses. Simply grate and mix in.

HERBS

Herbs can be added to mash. Adding spring onion makes the Irish dish called 'champ', while added cabbage or kale makes 'colcannon'.

Roast potatoes

A key part of Sunday lunch, but also so good they're worth making midweek, roast potatoes should be golden and crunchy on the outside and soft and fluffy on the inside. Here's how I make mine.

INGREDIENTS

For 4–6 people: allow a large potato per person
- 4–6 Maris Piper or King Edward potatoes
- 100g lard
- A few pinches of sea salt

I find fresh Maris Pipers or King Edwards work best. If you've got spuds that have been knocking about the cupboard for a few weeks (don't ever put potatoes in the fridge, it turns them gritty), I find they don't crisp up as well. Fine to use in mash though.

A word about the cooking fat used, I think the best roasties – or chips for that matter – are cooked in animal fats: either lard, goose fat or beef dripping. I just think they give a better colour and flavour to the finished spud.

EXTRA FLAVOURS

If you want to play around with some additional flavours like rosemary or garlic, put these in the pan when you first melt the fat to infuse, but remove them before adding the potatoes, as they'll burn during the cooking process.

METHOD

1 Peel the potatoes and chop any large ones into chunks. Cutting on a slant means you're increasing the size of the surface area of the potato meaning more of it can be exposed to the heat and oil in the tray.

2 Heat the oven to 200°C. Par-boil the potatoes in water until the edges are just beginning to break up and go soft.

3 Melt your lard in the roasting tray you're going to use.

4 You want to dry out your par-boiled potatoes as much as possible. You can speed up this process by placing the colander of potatoes in the oven for a few minutes (obviously don't do this if you've got a plastic one and remember to use oven gloves when removing it).

5 Tip the melted fat out of the tin into a mug, then add the potatoes to the tin.

6 Using a pastry brush, or just by gently pouring over, apply fat to each potato. Doing it this way means you can judge fat levels correctly – and you're not shaking the tray to coat them, splashing boiling fat over your hob and wrists.

7 Sprinkle over some salt and return to the oven for 40 minutes. Potatoes need a high heat to get a good crispy edge.

Yorkshire puddings

A must when serving roast beef (see page 91) and not too hard to make. You can make individual ones, or one large one that you cut up at the table to share. Make the batter in a stand mixer, a food processor or with a hand whisk, but however you do it, make sure you rest it in the fridge for at least 20 minutes (or longer) before adding to the hot fat.

You should only put your Yorkies in once your meat has come out to rest. You need a really high heat to get a rise, and this last burst of heat can also help finish off your roasties too.

INGREDIENTS

- 4 eggs
- 600ml milk
- 250g plain flour
- Large pinch of salt
- 100g lard

METHOD

1 Crack the eggs into a bowl and beat, then add the milk, flour and seasoning and whisk until fully combined. You're after something with the viscosity of cream.
2 Turn the oven up to 220°C.
3 Place teaspoons of the lard in each of the holes of the tin and put in the oven to melt. You want it almost smoking (about 5 minutes). Get the batter out of the fridge and have a ladle ready.
4 Working quickly, take the tin from the oven and put a ladle of batter in each hole. It should fizz and bubble at the edges. Return to the oven and bake for about 25–30 minutes until puffed up and golden brown.

Proper gravy

Rather than a light, clear, flavourful sauce to anoint our meat, gravy seems to have become opaque, thick-as-gloss-paint and gloopy these days. Well, I think that's wrong. Gravy is a sauce; it is not 'brown custard'.

Gravy granules may save time but I think they taste horrible and contain little more than starch, a caramel brown food colouring (E150c) and salt. To paraphrase the old nautical saying, 'you don't want to spoil the meat for a ha'peth of gravy'. 'What about gravy browning?' you ask. Well it's a complete waste of money too: it basically consists of our old friend E150c, salt and glucose.

Stocks made from leftover bones (see pages 168–169) are the key to good gravy. Just take one out the freezer, pop in a small saucepan, and heat up.

INGREDIENTS
Serves 4
- 500ml stock
- 1 teaspoon of plain flour
- 1 tablespoon of water
- Salt and pepper

METHOD
Thickening gravy
Gravy will thicken by itself as it reduces; the downside with this is that as it does so, it reduces the amount of gravy you have left to serve. Fine for one or two, but not enough to go round a table rammed with extended family for Sunday lunch. You could double up the amount, or use a small amount of plain flour to thicken your stock, so as to keep the volume. Do not put the flour straight into the hot gravy, however – it'll just turn to lumps and ruin it. Instead put a teaspoon of the flour in a tea cup and add a tablespoon of cold water.

Mix this together until the flour has dissolved. It should look like thin cream. Now, add one teaspoon to your gravy and stir. It'll take a few moments to cook and start to thicken your sauce, you'll need to bring it up to the boil then down to a simmer. It may be that one teaspoon is enough but if it's not, add another teaspoon. Judge by eye and remember to taste it – if it tastes powdery, you need to cook out the flour a bit more.

WHAT ABOUT CORNFLOUR?
Saint Delia of Norwich says cornflour gives a gloopy texture, and if you use too much, it will. It's much 'stronger' than plain flour, so you need much less. Cornflour is best used to thicken your sauce inside a pie, rather than thicken a gravy.

ADDITIONAL FLAVOURS

Serving separate gravy lets you add additional flavours that will complement your food. Here are some popular ones:

- **RED WINE** – A glug of red wine in your stock will add a richer note; the booze will cook out. Let it reduce for a bit longer, and go easy on any other thickenings. Best for beef dishes.
- **WHITE WINE** – As above, best served with things like chicken.
- **Other booze** – Port, beer and masala can all be added too. I'd steer clear of lager, spirits and alcopops, mind.
- **REDCURRANT JELLY** – This adds a sharper citrus note to gravy.
- **MUSTARD** – A teaspoon of Dijon mustard gives gravy a real kick.
- **ONIONS** – Onion gravy is great, but you need to chop the onions finely into small pieces and sweat them right down – I'm talking 30 minutes or more – on a very, very low heat, before adding your frozen stock. Adding a pinch of salt draws out the moisture and will help them break down faster; you consequently don't need to season at the end. Some finely chopped garlic wouldn't hurt either.

SEASONING
Remember, we didn't add salt to the stock when making it, so now's the time to check the seasoning for your gravy. A couple of twists of pepper and a pinch of salt at the end will see it right.

ANOTHER WAY TO MAKE GRAVY
If you want a thicker, more opaque gravy, don't reach for the gravy granules. Make a roux by mixing flour with melted butter, but instead of adding milk add your stock. Heat and stir until thickened, adding more stock if necessary. This will give a very light, tan-coloured gravy, what I call 'American' gravy. It goes particularly well with turkey.

A WORD ABOUT GRAVY BOATS
In times past, to pour gravy directly onto your food from the sauce boat would have marked you out as uncouth. Sauce boats always came with a spoon or ladle that allowed you, or more likely the servant waiting on you, to ladle one or two spoons of sauce over your food. The spout on a sauce boat was where the ladle rested.

Somewhere between the end of World War One and the invention of Bisto, the gravy spoon went missing in the cutlery drawer of history, but if you want the full Downton experience buy a sauce spoon for your gravy boat. It's the proper way to do it.

Homemade baked beans

Allegedly, the famous food writer Jane Grigson once asked a friend what she should give her children for tea. 'What about baked beans?' said her friend. 'Oh but they take so long to make!' she replied. She's right, they do take a while to make from scratch, but it's not like you've got to stand over them fussing and they're so much better than those out of a tin. Here's my version: they're as great on a huge butter-soaked slab of toasted sourdough as they are on a baked spud (which you can cook at the same time as the beans).

I think the secret to making great-tasting baked beans is molasses or black treacle. It has the sweetness, but also that dark, rich, sticky taste. This recipe will make loads, which you can easily freeze. I'm using whole plum tomatoes, which I've blitzed in a jug with a stick blender as they're less watery than chopped tinned tomatoes. You could also use a carton of passata.

INGREDIENTS

- 1 tin of plum tomatoes, blitzed up
- Knob of butter
- 100g smoked lardons
- 1 onion, finely chopped
- 2 tins of haricot beans, drained
- Salt and pepper
- 1 teaspoon of cayenne or paprika
- 1 tablespoon of treacle

BEAN FACTS

- Native Americans would eat beans and pulses stewed in bear fat with maple syrup. This inspired European settlers in New England to create their own versions using pork belly and treacle.
- When Henry J Heinz first brought his tinned beans to Britain in 1886, they were a luxury and sold exclusively at Fortnum & Mason in London for around £1.50 in today's money.

METHOD

1 Heat the oven to 150°C. (Place your potatoes in now if you're making baked spuds too).
2 Blitz the tomatoes in a high-sided jug and set aside.
3 Melt the butter in a pan and add the lardons. Cook on a low heat until much of the fat has been rendered out.
4 Add the onions and cook until soft.
5 Add the drained cans of beans, the blitzed tomato, seasoning, and cayenne or paprika and stir.
6 Add the treacle last and continue gently stirring. (If you leave it, the treacle can sink and stick to the bottom of the pan, as I and a now-discarded pan found to our cost!)
7 When it's at a simmer, place in the oven and leave for an hour. You can give it the odd stir to break the skin and combine. Leave to cool for 10 minutes before serving.

TIP

You can also use dried beans for this recipe: just soak overnight in cold water. The next day, place the beans in fresh water in a saucepan and bring to a boil for 10 minutes, then add to the recipe above when the tinned ones are added.

Rubs, pastes and marinades

Rubs, pastes and marinades let you add extra flavours to your meat. Don't go mad, though; they should enhance and support the flavour of the meat, not drown it out in a mouth-burning bonanza of heat and spice. Pick a few flavours that complement the meat you're working with, and stick with those.

MARINADE FLAVOURINGS

Common additions are:
- Orange, lemon or lime juice
- Apple, papaya or pineapple juice
- Mustard
- Maple syrup
- Honey
- Treacle
- Ketchup, or other sauce such as soy

Upping the liquid content still further gives you a marinade:
- Milk or yoghurt
- Wine
- Beer or cider
- Fruit juice
- Cola

DRY RUBS

As the name suggests, dry rubs are made from dry ingredients and help give an extra flavour coating to meat when it's cooking. They tend to have a stronger flavour than marinades.

A rough rule of thumb is to allow 3–4 tablespoons of rub per 500g of meat.

Dry rub tips
- Rub the mixture firmly into the meat.
- The longer you can leave it, the better it'll be – but don't leave the rub on too long. Half a day or overnight is good.

- Don't cook rubbed meat over too high a heat, as the spices will burn and turn bitter.
- Remove any excess rub with a pastry brush or a good shake.
- Don't overdo it and add the whole spice rack. Pick a dominant flavour and then support it with a few extras.

WETTER RUBS, PASTES AND MARINADES

You can also make wetter rubs or pastes by adding a little liquid. If you're going to baste the meat with the marinade as it cooks,

don't use the one it's just sat in, otherwise you'll be putting liquid that's had raw meat in it onto cooked meat. Instead, make two batches: one for marinating and the other for basting. That way your guests avoid salmonella.

DRY RUB FLAVOURINGS

Here are some suggestions for flavourings to experiment with:

BEEF	PORK	LAMB
Mustard powder	Fennel seeds	Rosemary
Chilli powder	Cumin	Mint
Star anise	Sage	Thyme
Garlic powder	Five spice	Lavender (honestly!)
Blitzed, dried mushrooms	Sugar	Chilli
Curry powder	Orange zest	Paprika
Coffee	Cinnamon	Anchovies
	Pineapple and apple juice	Turmeric

Flavoured butters and sauces

Like rubs and marinades, flavoured butters and sauces shouldn't overpower the meat you're serving. After all, roast beef needs gravy, but shouldn't be swimming in it. Butters are designed to melt and glaze your hot meat, releasing herbs or other flavourings as they do so.

FLAVOURED BUTTERS

Flavoured butters are really easy to make, here's how:

METHOD

1 Buy a good-quality slightly salted butter and bring to room temperature.
2 Beat in a bowl with a spoon and add your flavourings.
3 Scoop out and form the butter into a rough sausage shape.
4 Place onto a sheet of baking paper or cling film and roll to ensure an even surface.
5 Chill in the fridge. When needed remove a little of the cling film and slice a 1cm disc off for each person.

You can experiment with lots of different flavours in various amounts. The following guidelines assume around 120g of softened butter, which should give you enough to top 4 steaks or pieces of meat.

Maitre d'Hotel butter
A classic. To the softened butter add: 1 teaspoon of lemon juice, 1 teaspoon of chopped fresh parsley, 1 teaspoon of Dijon mustard, a pinch of paprika and salt and pepper.

Tarragon butter
Great with chicken, as well as meaty white fish. Add 1 teaspoon of lemon juice, 1 tablespoon of finely chopped tarragon and salt and pepper. You can also add a very small amount of garlic, if you wish.

Horseradish butter
Great on steaks and chops. Add 1 tablespoon of quality horseradish to the softened butter, or alternatively used freshly grated, along with salt and pepper.

Chilli butter
Use on grilled lamb chops. Finely dice or blitz a deseeded fresh chilli

and mix with the softened butter. Add finely chopped coriander and a squeeze of lime juice.

Anchovy butter
An unusual variation that works surprisingly well with lamb. To the butter add 3 finely chopped tinned anchovies and a small bunch of parsley. Alternatively use a teaspoon of Gentleman's relish.

Italian butter
Add finely diced sun-dried tomatoes, basil and a tablespoon of grated Parmesan to the butter.

SAUCES

Chimichurri
A green sauce from Argentina, served with grilled meats. It's made from finely chopped parsley, minced garlic, olive oil, oregano and white wine vinegar. The Uruguayan version adds chilli flakes.

Mayonnaise
Homemade mayo is so much better than shop-bought, but do use free-range or organic eggs, as you're adding the yolks raw. Put 2 egg yolks in a bowl and slowly drizzle in 250ml of neutral oil, such as sunflower. Add a teaspoon of mustard, a tablespoon of something acidic such as lemon juice or white wine vinegar, and season well with salt. Great with cold chicken.

Mint sauce
Synonymous with lamb. Finely chop a large bunch of fresh mint, place in a bowl and add 2 tablespoons of caster sugar. Pour over 2–3 tablespoons of boiling water and stir to dissolve the sugar. Add 2 tablespoons of red wine vinegar and leave to cool.

Cumberland sauce
Named after the Duke of Cumberland, though part of a long tradition of fruity sauces going back to the Middle Ages. Zest an orange and a lemon into a pan, just cover with water and bring to the boil to remove any bitterness. Then add the juice of the orange, a glass of port, two glasses of red wine, a pinch of ginger, 1 tablespoon of Dijon mustard, 2 tablespoons of caster sugar and 3 tablespoons of redcurrant jelly.

CHAPTER 9
LEFTOVERS, STOCKS AND SAUCES

I am very much a fan of leftovers and believe you should always cook more than you need. Going 'large' at the weekend means you don't have to do too much cooking for the following few days. Time changes cooked dishes in subtle ways. All the hot, busy flavours of a roast, stew or even a curry calm down and taste different the next day – more in tune, mellower in the mouth, perhaps.

Of course, one of the most enjoyable things about leftovers is eating straight from the fridge. I'm sure I'm not the only person who's reached for the milk to make a late night cuppa and found myself tearing a strip off a chicken carcass or holding a cold roast potato.

The following chapter contains not only dishes that can be made to see you through the next few days, but also meat stocks that can, with the help of the freezer, make tasty meals for the next few weeks. Remember, you should only reheat meat once.

Bubble and squeak

This can *only* be made with leftovers – only a fool would set out to make it from scratch. While leftover meat gets a range of treatments, from pies to curries, leftover veggies are lucky if they have a brief stay of execution in the fridge before hitting the recycling bin a few days later – this is the dish that gives them a royal pardon.

A quick word on the name for those of you that don't know, it's bubble and squeak because that's the noise it's said to make during cooking as the air heats up and squeezes out and the gravy warms up and starts to bubble.

You've got a lot of options with this recipe, depending on what your leftovers consist of; from the classic British bubble to something more like a Spanish frittata with the addition of any eggs you've got. You can get creative with shape and even apply a coating of breadcrumbs.

Let's start, however, with a more traditional version. I like a firmer slice of bubble, more like a fishcake than the traditional looser arrangement, and so have added a handful of breadcrumbs (stale bread blitzed in a mini food processor). I think the addition of an egg also helps to bind the mixture together.

INGREDIENTS

Serves 2–4, you could always bulk out with a side of buttered bread or baked beans

- 4 tablespoons of mashed potato (if you have leftover roast potatoes, just mash them up with a fork)
- 1–2 tablespoons of leftover cabbage, finely chopped
- 3 tablespoons of butter
- 1 egg
- Handful of soft breadcrumbs
- Any other vegetables you have, such as peas and chopped carrots
- Salt and pepper

METHOD

1 Prepare all the ingredients and add to a mixing bowl. With clean hands, combine together to ensure a good even mixture. You want it slightly firm, as it will loosen when cooking.

2 Scoop up the mixture and shape it into balls before squashing them flat with your hands to make patties. You could also use a scone cutter or small ring. Repeat until all the mixture is used. Don't make them too thick: no more than 2cm.

3 In a large frying pan or pancake pan, melt 150g of butter and swirl around.

4 Add each 'bubble cake' to the pan on a gentle heat, ensuring they don't touch. Fry for about 10 minutes. When your nose and a little lift and peak tells you they're crispy and golden brown on one side, flip over with a fish slice and cook the other side.

5 Leave to cool a little before serving.

BIGGER BUBBLE

I've made individual bubble and squeaks, but if you've got a small 9cm frying pan you can make a larger one to share. The knack is: a) knowing when the underside is done, and b) getting it out of the pan by placing a plate over the pan and turning it upside down. You then just gently slide it back into the pan to cook the top. Alternatively, you could cover with cheese and finish under the grill. You can also make them in a Yorkshire pudding tray.

EXTRAS

The veg will be quite tired flavourwise, but you can help lift it by adding a few chopped soft herbs, such as parsley, fresh thyme, or tarragon to the mixture. Any grated remains of the contents of the cheese board would also work. Or you can add some punch at the end by serving with brown sauce, capers or a gherkin. Finally a poached or fried egg atop is a wonderful addition to bubble and squeak.

Venturing further afield, if you omit the cabbage and slice your roasties into discs, add finely chopped onion and some red peppers sweated down in the pan beforehand, as well as four beaten eggs, you have a tortilla. Chopping your leftover roasties into cubes and adding curry spices and some wilted fresh spinach will give you sag aloo.

Beef stock

It's always worth buying beef on the bone if you can. Yes, you'll pay extra at the till, as the bone weighs more (though most butchers take this into account and charge more for off-the-bone, as they have to remove it and they're then also left with a bone to dispose of). It provides not only flavour and structure during the initial cooking, but also helps to make amazing stock.

INGREDIENTS

Makes about 2 litres

- Some beef bones – whatever you can get your hands on, the more the merrier. Any beef trimmings, and if you really want to, any beef bits left on your household plates.
- 2 large carrots
- 2 sticks of celery
- 1 large onion
- Parsley, including stalks (optional)
- 6 peppercorns
- 1 'petal' from a star anise
- 2 bay leaves
- 3 litres of water

If you strike up a friendship with your butcher, (not an easy task, take it slowly and go early or midweek), he may even give you some bones for free. It helps if you buy something else too, don't just walk in and demand bones.

For beef stock, I like to add one single petal from a star anise. Trust me, this'll give an extra subtle flavour to the stock, but won't overpower it.

If you want a really dark stock or your bones are fresh from your new best mate the butcher, you might want to roast them first. Put the oven on full whack and pop them in to brown for 15 minutes.

METHOD

1 **The hob method:** Place all the ingredients in a large pan and pour over a kettle of freshly boiled water. Top up with cold water if needed. Put on a low heat on the back burner and leave it, lid off, for 4–5 hours minimum, or longer if you've got time. It's even better if done overnight.

    The oven method: Put your stock in the oven on a low heat (say 60ºC) overnight. Your kitchen will smell amazing the next morning.

2 Once all the ingredients in the stock are looking like they've given all they have to give, strain and leave to cool, before decanting into containers.

Chicken stock

Throwing away a chicken carcass should be a crime, and it also adds insult to (the fatal) injury the poor chook you've just scoffed received. That bird's bones still have so much flavour to give you, rather than landfill, so make the most of it.

If you've no pressing need for chicken stock in your life right now, pop the carcass in the freezer until you're ready to put it with another one. A two-carcass stock will have much more flavour than a one-bird version. You might need to break up the birds to fit them in the pot.

Like beef, roasting the bones will give a darker colour and more robust flavour. If you're after something more delicate, use as is.

You can add more chicken reinforcements to your carcass: chicken wings are dead cheap and their high gelatine content makes for a great sticky, flavoursome stock.

INGREDIENTS
Makes about 1–1.5 litres
- 1 or 2 chicken carcasses
- 6 chicken wings (optional)
- 2 carrots, roughly chopped
- 1 stick of celery
- 6 whole peppercorns
- 2 bay leaves
- 2 large onions, quartered
- Small bunch of parsley stalks
- 2 litres of water

1 Place the ingredients in a large saucepan, add the water and bring to the boil, then turn to a low heat and simmer for 3 hours then strain and portion into containers.

Chicken stock another way
Once the stars aligned and fate delivered to me three *poulet de Bresse* chicken carcasses. These are some of the most pampered chickens in the world, living long happy lives in France – they're the Rolls-Royce of chickens.

Consequently this required a special treatment, so I did an overnight stock. This is exactly the same as above, but you place the pan in a low oven, around 90°C, to reduce overnight.

A remouillage
After you've strained your stock and the bones and veg have given their best, you can still produce a second-rate stock from them. The French call this a *remouillage*. It won't be as strong or flavoursome as the first stock, but it does have uses.

A double stock
You can turn the 'chicken-ness' up to 11 with this technique. Instead of adding two litres of water to your carcasses, you add two litres of a previously made chicken stock. Cook it in exactly the same way as above, strain and enjoy. This is where the *remouillage*, outlined above, comes in perfectly.

Additions
Of course, the above recipe is just for a basic stock; you can always tweak flavours depending on your intended final use. So, try adding herbs such as tarragon, sage leaves and rosemary. If you're using your stock in a spicier context, then chuck in a sliced fresh chilli and maybe a thumb-sized piece of fresh ginger. You could also replace the parsley with coriander. Finally any dregs of white wine you've got left over can also be added.

Other birds
Pheasants, duck and turkey can all be made into stock. You might have trouble finding a pan big enough to take a turkey carcass whole, so break it up and just use half, freezing the other half for later.

Soups

Not so much a recipe here as a set of suggestions. Leftover meat – and indeed veggies – along with stock can be re-fashioned into new dishes the next day.

CHICKEN AND SWEETCORN

Add fresh, frozen, or even tinned sweetcorn to any scraps of meat along with a sweated down onion and stock made from the carcass. Season well. A blob of crème fraîche or a splash of cream wouldn't go amiss too. Blitz a little before serving.

THAI STYLE BROTH

To a dark, clear chicken stock, add any leftover shredded meat, a splash of Thai fish sauce, chopped coriander and bird's eye chilli. You can up the veggie count with the likes of pak choi, sugar snap peas or green beans. A squeeze of lime juice wouldn't hurt either. Can also be made with leftover beef.

RAMEN

There are many variations of this Japanese dish, but they all feature a good stock as a base. Then it's just a question of adding any of the following: noodles, leftover meat, beansprouts, spring onion, chilli, greens and finally a soft-boiled egg.

SOUP TIPS

- If you want to thicken a vegetable soup quickly, finely grate in a small amount of potato.
- Nearly every good European-style soup starts with finely diced onions, carrots, celery and garlic.
- Asian-style soups by and large tend to have stronger flavours added like miso, soy and fish sauce, along with spices. If you're planning on making Asian-style soups, make your chicken or pork stock not with onions, carrots and celery, but ginger, leek and chilli.
- Soups are essentially about vegetables, meat and some form of carbohydrate (pasta, rice, pulses) combined and cooked in a good stock. Consequently, pretty much anything goes (though I once had lamb and pasta soup in a pub and it was utterly disgusting).
- Soups can be 'topped' with ingredients to add a different texture and interesting appearance. Think fresh herbs, slugs of oil, sprinkles of seeds or crumbled cheese.

COCK-A-LEEKIE

Traditionally, cock-a-leekie soup is thickened with rice, but I prefer using finely diced potato. Simply cook in chicken stock until tender, then add any leftover meat and lastly the finely shredded leeks

(green and white parts). Finely sliced prunes are the other traditional topping. Cock-a-leekie was one of two soups available on the Titanic's lunch menu the day it sank, fact fans.

FRENCH ONION SOUP

You need a good amount (around 1litre) of rich, dark beef stock to make this soup, so make sure you roast the bones prior to making the stock. The other main ingredient is onions, and lots of them (over 1kg). Cook slowly in butter until they begin to break down and caramelise. A pinch of brown sugar towards the end helps them along. Add garlic, a tablespoon of flour, and a splash of cognac, Madeira or dark sherry. Then add the hot beef stock and reduce. Serve with slices of baguette topped with melted cheese.

MULLIGATAWNY

Finely dice onion, celery, garlic, ginger and chilli and soften in a pan with some vegetable oil. Add red split lentils, two teaspoons of curry powder, and any beef or chicken stock you have then cook until the lentils are soft. Add a little coconut milk and blitz until smooth. Serve with finely shredded chilli, a blob of yoghurt and coriander.

MINESTRONE

Dice or shred the following in a food processor: onion, carrot, stick of celery, a quarter of a cabbage and a potato. Soften in a pan with some vegetable oil, then add a good amount of stock and a tin of cannellini or borlotti beans and gently cook for 20 minutes. If you've an old Parmesan cheese rind lying about, add that too (it'll melt, remove before serving). Finally, add small pasta shapes, broken up pieces of spaghetti, or risotto rice, and cook for a further 20 minutes until the pasta or rice is cooked. Check the seasoning and serve. Let's be clear about this, it isn't gourmet eating, it's a big comforting bowl of soft veggies and filling carbs.

THE CURIOUS TALE OF BROWN WINDSOR SOUP

This soup has a peculiar history. Many think it a Victorian classic, straight from the pages of Mrs Beeton. In fact, it seems to have been invented in the 1940s for cultural, rather than culinary effect and appears in novels and radio plays of the period as a pejorative term used to describe the sort of dreadful food found in many post-war guest houses and hotels in Britain. There are 19th-century recipes for soups called *Potage a la Windsor,* as well as a white Windsor soup, not to mention Brown Windsor soup. Incidentally, the current royal family didn't change their name from Saxe-Coburg-Gotha to Windsor until 1917, after the unfortunate business with Germany.

Final thoughts, facts and suppliers

BEEF AND LIBERTY

In the mid 18th century, beef steak clubs were formed by notable gentlemen of the day. Membership included prime ministers, actors, artists, bishops, soldiers and royalty. They ate steaks and baked potatoes, which were accompanied by port or porter, after which there was talk, song and revelry. The most famous, The Sublime Society of Beef Steaks, was founded in 1735 and ran until 1867. Members wore a uniform and the insignia was a gridiron, which bore the phrase, 'beef and liberty'.

DROVING

Droving is the art of walking cattle from one region to another. In pre-industrial times cattle were 'droved' from the pastures and hills of Scotland as far south as London.

USEFUL WEB LINKS

PRODUCERS
www.freerangepork.co.uk
www.dingleydell.com
suttonhoochicken.co.uk
freerangebirds.co.uk
www.donaldrussell.com
www.cureandsimple.com
www.cabrito.co.uk
www.wildmeat.co.uk

BUTCHERS AND FARM SHOPS
www.qguild.co.uk
www.thegingerpig.com
www.newlyns-farmshop.co.uk
gogmagoghills.com

OTHER RESOURCES
www.simplybeefandlamb.co.uk
www.lovepork.co.uk
www.deliciousmagazine.co.uk

BUTCHERY COURSES
www.schoolofartisanfood.org
courses.rivercottage.net

Drovers were men of character; they passed news, information and money around the country. One drover, David Jones, set up a bank in Llandovery in 1799 to help Welsh drovers, and took the black ox as its symbol. It was eventually taken over by Lloyds in 1909.

ROYAL ROAST OX

In 1953, the Ministry of Food granted applications for communities to roast a whole oxen to celebrate the coronation, but only if they could prove that by tradition, an ox had been roasted at previous coronations. (154 applications were received; of those 40 were withdrawn, 33 refused and 81 approved.)

BEEFEATERS

Officially known as The Yeomen Warders of Her Majesty's Royal Palace and Fortress the Tower of London, and Members of the Sovereign's Body Guard of the Yeoman Guard Extraordinary. History does not accurately relate why they have the nickname 'beefeater', but the most commonly held view is that they were paid in, or indeed ate a lot of, beef. Today, one of their members, the Ravenmaster, is responsible for the feeding of the ravens at the tower (legend has it that if the ravens leave the tower, the monarchy will crumble). The birds are fed a daily ration of raw beef bought from nearby Smithfield.
http://www.hrp.org.uk/tower-of-london/

LONDON'S GREAT MEAT MARKET

Smithfield is home to London's meat market, which dates back to the 10th century. Its name is thought to come from 'smooth field': a large, open area outside the medieval city walls and near the banks of the river Fleet, allowing cattle to be rested and traded.

Its current form was designed in the 19th century by Sir Horace Jones, with some hideous later architectural additions in the early 1990s. It is London's oldest wholesale market, operating from the same location since medieval times. It starts early, with many porters there in the small hours and – thanks to the congestion charge – it's all done by 7am. If you get up early, it's well worth a visit to see it before it's forced out, and members of the public can buy from there. It was here, in 1381, that peasant revolt leader Wat Tyler was killed while negotiating with King Richard II.
http://www.smithfieldmarket.com

Conversion tables

All these conversions are very close, but not necessarily accurate to several decimal points, so be careful. Also, many recipes (not ours) won't work if you mix imperial and metric, as the two use slightly different quantities. Beware. Also, the speed of light is exactly 299,792,458 metres per second. That might come in handy one day.

OVEN TEMPERATURES

Gas Mark	°C	°F
1	140°C	275°F
2	150°C	300°F
3	170°C	325°F
4	180°C	350°F
5	190°C	375°F
6	200°C	400°F
7	220°C	425°F
8	230°C	450°F
9	240°C	475°F

If using a fan oven you will need to reduce the oven temperature slightly (check your oven manual).

VOLUME

Imperial	Metric
2 fl oz	55 ml
3 fl oz	75 ml
5 fl oz (¼ pint)	150 ml
10 fl oz (½ pint)	275 ml
1 pint	570 ml
1 ¼ pint	725 ml
1 ¾ pint	1 litre
2 pint	1.2 litre
2½ pint	1.5 litre
4 pint	2.25 litre

WEIGHTS

Imperial	Metric
½ oz	10 g
¾ oz	20 g
1 oz	25 g
1½ oz	40 g
2 oz	50 g
2½ oz	60 g
3 oz	75 g
4 oz	110 g
4½ oz	125 g
5 oz	150 g
6 oz	175 g
7 oz	200 g
8 oz	225 g
9 oz	250 g
10 oz	275 g
12 oz	350 g
1 lb	450 g
1 lb 8 oz	700 g
2 lb	900 g
3 lb	1.35 kg

LIQUID CONVERSIONS

Imperial	Metric	American
½ fl oz	15 ml	1 tbsp
1 fl oz	30 ml	⅛ cup
2 fl oz	60 ml	¼ cup
4 fl oz	120 ml	½ cup
8 fl oz	240 ml	1 cup
16 fl oz	480 ml	1 pint

DIMENSIONS

Imperial	Metric
⅛ inch	3 mm
¼ inch	5 mm
½ inch	1 cm
¾ inch	2 cm
1 inch	2.5 cm
1¼ inch	3 cm
1½ inch	4 cm
1¾ inch	4.5 cm
2 inch	5 cm
2½ inch	6 cm
3 inch	7.5 cm
3½ inch	9 cm
4 inch	10 cm
5 inch	13 cm
5¼ inch	13.5 cm
6 inch	15 cm
6½ inch	16 cm
7 inch	18 cm
7½ inch	19 cm
8 inch	20 cm
8½ inch	21.5 cm
9 inch	23 cm
9½ inch	24 cm
10 inch	25.5 cm
11 inch	28 cm
12 inch	30 cm

INDEX